APPRECIATIONS

"Sometimes a person touches your life, teaches you things you realize you never knew, and cracks your heart open to living and loving in a way you never were before. Thank you, Lisa, for being that person." —TERI

"You always know just what to say and how to say it. Your posts touch us in ways you can't know." —ERIKA

"Thank you for articulating such difficult thoughts and emotions in such a remarkably clear and beautiful way." —A. MEADE

"Your postings are so powerful and have come to mean so much to me. You give me insight and a sense that I am not alone." —JENNIFER

"Your words express what we feel but cannot put into words." —DARLENE

"Your reflections on life, love, loss, grief and family help me to get through my tough days." —ANONYMOUS

"You are equipping women to be braver, stronger, real and better able to face and deal with what needs to be overcome." —MARCI

PERSEVERE:
A LIFE WITH CANCER

REFLECTIONS ON LOVE AND LOSS, FAMILY AND
FRIENDSHIP, COMPASSION AND COURAGE

LISA BONCHEK ADAMS

CURATED BY HER MOTHER AND BROTHER,
DRS. RITA AND MARK BONCHEK

ISBNs: 978-0-9991629-0-3 (paperback); 978-0-9991629-1-0 (ePub); 978-0-9991629-2-7 (Kindle);

Library of Congress Catalog Number: 2017910861
Printed in the United States of America
First Printing: 2017
21 20 19 18 17   5 4 3 2 1

Cover and interior design by Ryan Scheife, Mayfly Design

For permission requests, please address:
The Bonchek Family Foundation
400 Willow Valley Square
Suite GA-410
Lancaster, PA 17602

Proceeds from sales of this book will fund research into finding a cure for metastatic breast cancer.

To donate, order books or learn more about Lisa's work, please visit www.LisasBook.com.

DEDICATION

In loving memory of Lisa Bonchek Adams
and in honor of her husband, Clarke,
and their children Paige, Colin and Tristan.

"The words I have written will one day be a gift,
not to the children that they are,
but to the adults that I am raising them to be."

LISA BONCHEK ADAMS, DECEMBER 1, 2010

INTRODUCTION

By Drs. Rita and Mark Bonchek

Persevere: A Life with Cancer is for people living with cancer and those who love and care about them.

The book is an edited collection of writings by Lisa Bonchek Adams. Lisa died in 2015 from breast cancer at the age of 45. She was a devoted wife and mother. She was also a remarkably prolific and talented writer. Lisa had a gift for conveying the experience of cancer in a way that helped those with cancer feel understood, and those without cancer to understand. She simplified the complexities of treatment in a way that educated and informed. Through her, the uncomfortable and painful became approachable and accessible, without minimization or denial.

Lisa had more than an audience: she had a community. On Facebook, Twitter, and her blog, thousands of people sought Lisa's comfort and shared in her experience. They also supported each other. As Lisa said, "If you want to know what the future might be like, ask someone who has been there."

As her mother and brother, we are regularly approached by people who followed Lisa's writings. They tell us how much her writings meant to them, either as patients themselves or in helping them support others. They were hopeful Lisa would publish her work to make it easier to reference and to share.

Unfortunately, Lisa did not have enough time to publish her writings in print. To carry on Lisa's mission, we have curated Lisa's blog posts into this collection. We have selected the writings that best capture her voice, spirit, experience, and wisdom. They are arranged in a way we believe will tell her story and enable you to know her in the way that others did when she was alive.

Lisa's writings are truly timeless. We believe they will be as valuable today as when Lisa first wrote them. Be forewarned that some of the writings are not easy. But neither is cancer.

July 2017

"It is such a secret place, the land of tears."

ANTOINE DE SAINT-EXUPERY

CONTENTS

xi

WRITINGS

"Find a bit of beauty in the world today.
Share it. If you can't find it, create it.
Some days this may be hard to do.
Persevere."

Welcome

In December 2006, more than eight years ago, I heard the words, "You have cancer" for the first time.

I started writing about my experiences as a wife and young mother of three with breast cancer. I began by posting them on my Facebook page. Soon my friends were asking how their own friends and relatives could read my words. I was writing about the darker, richer emotions I was feeling—aimlessness, fear, despair—but also the dogged commitment to always be strong with an enthusiasm for life.

On my blog (www.lisabadams.com) and Twitter (@adamslisa), I wrote about death, life, family, sadness, joy, and sorrow. I thought it would only appeal to people with cancer, but I was wrong. Instead, the appeal has been far more universal. I receive emails from people who not only have had cancer themselves, but also those with family members who have had it. I hear from people who have experience with other illnesses, and also those who just want to know more about what it is like to confront mortality at an early age. The far-reaching emotional impact of illness affects many people, and they connect with my work.

In October of 2012 I learned that cancer had metastasized to my lymph nodes and bones and since that time has further metastasized to other sites. I now have stage IV breast cancer. Again I feel the need to communicate not only about the disease itself (true awareness) but also about its impact on my young family. My posts often give my insights into how to raise children who are resilient and can cope with inevitable hardship. The blog also will be a record of my love and devotion to my children. There is nowhere I would rather be than here with them.

I started this website to allow public access to my writings. I keep a blog here as well as some of my more popular essays and poems. This is creative writing informed by my personal and academic background; I examine the emotions of life-changing events.

My parents' careers have indelibly shaped my insights. My father, a (retired) heart surgeon, gave me a shrewd eye for detail and an aptitude for processing medical information. My mother, a (retired) psychologist specializing in grief, loss, death, and dying, shared insight into the mind of the bereaved family member. My own academic background includes a graduate degree in sociology. Combining medical, psychological, and sociological sensibilities has resulted in a unique way of experiencing and describing cancer and other traumatic life experiences.

I am pleased so many people have connected to the emotions I try to capture in my writing. I hope you will, too.

Is It Wrong to Be Sad on Christmas?: Mourning the Life I Thought I'd Have

(Three weeks after my salpingo-oophorectomy and two years after my diagnosis of breast cancer. This was the first blog post I ever wrote.)

I've only cried once today. That's not too bad. But the day is not yet done. Today, again, I'm thinking of the things that cancer has taken from me. First, let me say that I am well aware of the blessings I have. I remember them each and every minute of every day. They are what keep me going, keep me fighting. But today, again, I'm pulled into what's gone, what's irretrievable, what's changed.

The body parts are gone, of course. My feeling of immortality. Of safety, of security. I'm vulnerable now. And I feel it. Part of me wants to blaze down I-95 at 100 miles an hour because I've stared down cancer, so what can touch me now? Taking risks is a popular grief reaction. On the other hand, a part of me wants to curl up in bed and not come out.

Today, on Christmas, when the childlike wonder is all around, I feel like I am watching it from high above me, as it happens TO ME, around me. I smile, I do what I am supposed to do, I play the "Santa game" with my children. I eat delicious food. I gather up the gift wrap strewn about the living room. I pile the presents in the kids' rooms. I pack their suitcases for their 3:30 a.m. wakeup for their winter vacation. Half my family is leaving me tomorrow. They'll be back, of course, but they are leaving. And while they are gone I will ponder the sadness that has settled like a cloud since my latest surgery almost a month ago.

I know I'll be fine . . . everyone tells me so, as if to will it to be that way. Even in my darkest moments I know it is only temporary. But I am angry at cancer. Angry at the bad twist of fate that makes me unable to travel this year, unable to be myself, unable to shake this feeling that the dark cloud just seems to keep following me, like those creepy paintings in the museum whose eyes seem to follow your every move.

And knowing the other people who are similarly sad today, those who are remembering loved ones lost, and those who are suffering in pain, and those who will head in for more chemo and surgery and therapies before the year is out are also forever changed by the great equalizer of cancer.

To anyone who reads this and thinks it sounds so odd, so foreign—something that happens to "someone else"—I am so happy for you. I am jealous of you. I remember that feeling, but I am almost getting to the point where I am unable to remember it. I never thought it would be me thinking this way, feeling this way. But it is me. And it's taking a long time to grieve for that life I thought I would have.

Maybe that's what it is.
I'm in mourning.
I'm mourning the life I thought I would have.
And only time can help that.

December 25, 2008

Perspective

I never wrote about cancer when I was diagnosed.
I never wrote about my body before the surgeon cut into it.
I never wrote about chemo when I was going through it.
I never wrote about dying when I was most afraid.

This morning I was angry at myself. Why didn't I write during these times? Why didn't I capture the raw emotion as it was happening? Why did I let this emotional gold mine slip through my fingers?

First, of course, was the pain. When I was in physical pain, I couldn't be analytical. I couldn't be intelligent. I couldn't even be upright. When that pain dulled, and I started to feel better, I didn't want to be self-indulgent. I didn't want to think about me anymore. When I felt well, I wanted to be with my family. I wanted to give my children everything I had when I had it. I didn't want to take time away from them, sit in my office, and write.

So I waited.

What have I gained from waiting? By writing about past experiences, am I living in the past, dwelling on it, and anchoring myself to a difficult stage of my life?

No, I quickly thought. I'm not.

In fact, it is only now that I can look at the past four years clearly. Now that the pain of recovery has shifted I can see it for what it was—for what it is.

Only now can I put the past in perspective. But what does "having perspective" really mean?

Being in the right spot makes all of the objects in your vision align properly, in correct proportion to one another. If the perspective is "off" it means you're not viewing it from the right place.

Without perspective, your point of view is literally wrong.

What's changed? The objects you are looking at haven't changed. Your stance relative to them has. And in looking at the same objects from a different place, you see them differently. When we put life experiences in perspective, we are doing the same thing. By taking a few steps back, putting some distance between us and our experiences, we are better observers, we are more accurate.

My point of view was wrong before. When I was ticking off the boxes of surgeries, procedures, and treatments I was "too close" to them in space and time. Had I written about them then, I would have remembered more details of conversations, dates, and my surroundings. But that's not what I feel passionately about. I don't write about what it's like to go through these things as they happen.

Columnist Gene Weingarten writes, "A writer has to figure out what that piece is before she can begin to report her story. Only then can she know what questions to ask and what things to notice; only then will she see how to test her thesis and how to change it if it is wrong. That's what nonfiction storytelling is about. It is not enough for you to observe and report: You must also think."

I love to write about what life is like after these events happen— after you live through them and come out the other side . . . how you go on after, and what it feels like when you look back.

I can see this part more clearly because my emotions are separated from the pain, from the chaos, from the shock.

For a moment I regretted that I didn't write about all of this while it was happening. Now I know it was the right thing to do for me. Only now, with a bit of distance, can I put it all in perspective.

August 10, 2011

I Think So Too

That chair you're sitting in?

I've sat in it too.

In waiting rooms. Chemo rooms. Prep rooms. For tests. Surgeries. Procedures. Inpatient. Outpatient. Emergency visits. Routine visits. Urgent visits.

To see generalists. Specialists. Surgeons. Alone. With friends. With family members. As a new patient. Established patient. Good news. Bad news.

I've left with new scars. Prescriptions. Appointments. Words of wisdom. Theories. Guesses. Opinions. Statistics. Charts. Plans. Tests. Words of assurance. More bloodwork. Nothing new. Nothing gained. Nothing but a bill.

That feeling you're having?

I've had it too.

Shock. Disbelief. Denial. Grief. Anger. Frustration. Numbness. Sadness. Resignation. Confusion. Consternation. Curiosity.

Determination. Dread. Anxiety. Guilt. Regret. Loss. Pain. Emptiness. Embarrassment. Shame. Loneliness.

That day you're dreading?

I've dreaded it too.

The first time you speak the words, "I have cancer." The first time you hear "Mommy has cancer."

The day you wear a pink shirt instead of a white shirt. Anniversary day. Chemo day. Surgery day. Scan day. Decision day. Baldness day. The day the options run out.

Those reactions you're getting?

I've had them too.

Stares. Questions. Pity. Blank looks. Insensitivity. Jaw-dropping comments.

Those side effects you dread?

I've dreaded them too.

Nausea. Vomiting. Pain. Broken bones. Weakened heart. Baldness. Hair loss. Everywhere. Unrelenting runny nose. Fatigue. Depression. Hot flashes. Insomnia. Night sweats. Migraines. Loss of appetite. Loss of libido. Loss of breasts. Phantom pain. Infection. Fluid accumulation. Bone pain. Neuropathy. Numbness. Joint pain. Taste changes. Weight gain. Weight loss.

Some of them happen. Some don't. Eventually, though? You name it. It changes. Temporarily anyway.

That embarrassment you're feeling?

I've felt it too.

Buying a swimsuit. Getting a tight-fitting shirt stuck on my body in the dressing room. Having a child say, "You don't have any eyebrows, do you?" Wearing a scarf. Day after day. Wondering about wearing a wig because it's windy outside and it might not stay on.

That fear you're suppressing?

I've squelched it too.

Will this kill me? How bad is chemo going to be? How am I going to manage three kids and get through it? Will my cancer come back and take me away from my life? Will it make the quality of life I have left so bad I won't want to be here anymore? Is this pain in my back a recurrence? Do I need to call a doctor? If it comes back would I do any more chemo or is this as much fight as I've got in me? What is worse: the disease or the treatment?

That day you're yearning for?

I've celebrated it too.

"Your counts are good" day. "Your x-ray is clear" day. "Now you can go longer between appointments" day. "See you in a year" day. First-sign-of-hair day. First-day-without-covering-your-head day. First-taste-of-food day. First Monday-chemo-isn't-in-the-calendar day. Expanders-out, implants-in day. First-walk-without-being-tired day. First-game-of-catch-with-the-kids day. First-day-out-for-lunch-with-friends day. First-haircut day. "Hey, I went a whole day without thinking about cancer" day.

"Someone asked me how I'm doing, I said 'fine' and I meant it" day.

That hope you have?

I have it too:

A cure.

Don't you think that would be amazing?

I think so too.

April 27, 2009

Still the Best Policy: Being Honest with Your Children About Cancer

I met a woman who told me something shocking.

It wasn't that she'd had breast cancer.
Or had a double mastectomy with the TRAM flap procedure for reconstruction.
Or that she'd had chemotherapy.

What made my jaw literally drop open was her statement that she has never told the younger two of her four children that she's had cancer.

Ever.

Not when she was diagnosed.
Or recovering from any of her surgeries.
Or undergoing chemotherapy.

She never told them.
To this day—five years later—they do not know.

I like to think I'm pretty open-minded. But I confess, it took a lot of self-control not to blurt out, "I think that is a big mistake."

I'm a big believer in being open and honest with your children about having cancer. My caveat, using common sense, is that you should only give them age-appropriate information.

When I was diagnosed with breast cancer Tristan was six months old. Of course he didn't understand what cancer was. Colin, age five at the time, understood some of what was happening. I explained to him what cancer meant, that I was going to need surgery to take the cancer out, where the cancer was, what chemo was, what it would do to my appearance and energy level. Using words like "I will be more tired than I usually am. I might feel sick to my stomach and need to rest more" explained things in words he could understand.

Age eight and the oldest at the time, Paige understood the most when I was diagnosed. She had bigger questions as well as concerns about me ("Will I get it too? Who is going to take care of us? Are you going to be okay?").

It's not that I think small children always understand everything. But they are certainly able to sense that things are not "normal." They can tell when people are acting strange. I think it's important that they know there is a reason for that change.

Children have a tendency to be egocentric; they think that everything is their fault. They may think they have done something wrong if everything at home feels different.

The woman told me she didn't want to worry her children. She thought it "unnecessary" to tell them. She said when they got older she would explain it. I argue that by keeping her cancer a secret, she runs the risk of doing the opposite: making cancer seem scarier and more worrisome. (She decided to tell them that she was Christmas shopping, not staying in the hospital to recover from surgery. She made up reasons why her torso hurt and why she couldn't lift things.)

If children hear words like "cancer" casually in conversation as they grow up they will be comfortable with them; in that way, they won't be frightened of them. If they understand the truth of the diagnosis and treatment, they are dealing with reality. By hiding the truth, the unintended consequence is to make it seem worse than it is. By not telling children, and waiting until they are older, it reinforces the idea that cancer IS something "big and scary." After all, if it weren't, you would have told them already.

I think being secretive is a step backward to the days when cancer was only talked about in hushed tones: the "C" word or "a long illness." These concepts might seem primitive to us now, but it wasn't long ago that these vague labels were the norm. By showing our children, our friends, our neighbors that we can live with cancer, live after cancer, we put cancer in its rightful place.

To me, the deception that goes on to lie to children about where you are going, what you are doing is lying about a fundamental part of your life. Cancer isn't all I am—but it is a part. And it's an important part of my medical history. If for the past three years I'd covered up where I was going and what I was doing, the web of deceit would have been extensive. I can't (and won't) live a life like that.

Further, I think it's a poor example to set for my children.

Lying,
covering up information,
and omitting important information are all wrong.

With rare exception, the truth is always best.

Presented in the proper way,
commensurate with a child's age,
a difficult situation can be not only tolerable but surmountable.

It takes work. It takes parents who can manage not only their own emotions about having cancer but also be involved with helping their children cope with it. It's more work, but it's worth it.

I think that woman made a mistake. I think her decision was harmful. I am sure she thinks she was doing her children a favor. I totally disagree. I think keeping this type of information from children "in their own best interest" is rarely—if ever—the right thing to do.

April 9, 2010

While there may be exceptions, in general I firmly believe it's important to be open and honest with children about serious illness (in my case it was cancer). Not only is it important to explain it to them to de-mystify illness, it can also be crucial that children be aware of the condition in case of emergency. For example, if a child is alone with a parent who has a medical condition and the parent loses consciousness or injures herself, the child can call 911 and provide important information about what might be the cause for the problem. Similarly, people with metastatic cancer may have daily medical issues that are ongoing; chemotherapy that is chronic, repeat surgeries, severe side effects, and more frequent tests and appointments may mean hiding a diagnosis is probably not even an option. Metastatic cancer patients may view withholding information as a luxury they do not have.

Using the real words to name our diseases/conditions can also be important for children's knowledge of their family medical history. I have heard stories of women diagnosed with breast cancer who only learned of a family history of the disease after their own cancer was diagnosed. Only then did information come to light that relatives had also had the disease. Perhaps knowledge of a familial history of the disease would have been useful at an earlier time and monitoring could have begun sooner. (Usually screening recommendations are different if there is a family history.)

July 5, 2011

What If

What if I hadn't gone to the gynecologist on time for my six-month postpartum visit?

What if, during the breast exam, when my left breast felt "different" (no lump, no real reason, just "different") my doctor had dismissed it as post-nursing irregularity and told me to come back in six months for another exam?

What if, when I called to schedule the mammogram (only eighteen months after a clear one) and they said it would be a few months for an appointment I had said, "Okay"?

What if I hadn't called my doctor to tell her that's how long it would take and ask if that was acceptable?

What if she'd said, "Yes"?

What if I hadn't opted for a double mastectomy?

What if I hadn't gone for a second opinion on chemotherapy? What if I hadn't gotten a second pathologist to review my slides?

What if that didn't happen and I didn't find out with that second look that I actually had invasive ductal carcinoma in one breast, in my lymph node, and dysplastic cells in the other breast?

What if I had decided not to do those things? Where would I be now?

What if I hadn't been assertive, perceptive, inquisitive, impatient, and willing to do what it took to get answers?

I probably wouldn't be alive. Or if I were, I'd be spending my
time treating an advanced cancer.

Not blowing bubbles with Tristan today,
Not praising Colin for his schoolwork,
Not planning Paige's sleepover for tomorrow.

I wouldn't be able to enjoy the things I enjoyed today.

But I am here.
I was able to be with my family.
I was able to help others.
I am able to look to the future with hope.

And for that, I am happy.

March 18, 2011

The Mailbox

I went by my friend's house today—the one who was just
diagnosed with breast cancer. I wanted to put something in
her mailbox. When I opened the mailbox it was full of mail
already. She hadn't taken in yesterday's mail yet.

Of course she hadn't. Why should she worry about mail when
they are worrying about cancer and what it means for their
family?
I left the bag I brought in her mailbox on top of the day-old
mail and went away, remembering:

Remembering that time in my life two years ago when *I* was diagnosed with cancer.

I managed to get the kids where they needed to go (I have no idea where that was).

I did the things I needed to do (I have no memory of what they were).

I went the places I needed to go (I can't remember where they were).

There is no room for anything else in these days, these days in the beginning.

There is no room for anything else except to hear the words again and again,

as if you need to convince yourself that they are true: "You have cancer."

There is no room to
do anything,
think anything,
say anything,
be anything,
fear anything,
hope anything,
dream anything,
live anything,
love anything,
breathe anything.

In these days there is no room for anything but cancer.

But these days will pass.
You don't believe it.

Can't believe it.
But it's true:
these days will pass.

Your life will change.
You can make room for other things,
better things.

And once again,
there will be room in your mailbox.

You will remember to get the mail because you won't be think-
ing about cancer.
You'll be thinking about the things you should be thinking
about,
that you deserve to be thinking about.
Each day.
Every day.
Today.

July 18, 2009

Just Because

Just because you know someone who died from cancer doesn't
mean I will.

Just because you know someone who:

felt sick, felt great, felt tired, felt strong,
looked great, looked awful,
lost her hair, kept her hair,

ate healthy, ate crap,
took vitamins, ignored medical advice,
got acupuncture, believed in holistic medicine,

ate no soy, ate no sugar,
never laughed, never cried,

had surgery, had radiation, received chemotherapy,
got silicone implants, got saline implants,
had a great attitude, had a terrible attitude . . .

Just because you know someone who did

one of these things,
many of these things,
some of these things . . .

doesn't mean it will work for me.

It doesn't mean it will kill me.
It doesn't mean it will make me live.

Just because it worked for someone else doesn't mean it will
work for me.
It doesn't mean it won't. Or can't.

It might. It might not.

Just because you know someone who died from cancer doesn't
mean I will.

March 9, 2011

21

Promises You Can't Keep

Today I'm ranting. I decided my pieces fall into three categories: rants, raves, and reflections.

Today's rant is about promises you can't keep. Those of us who have cancer (had cancer—perhaps a meaningless distinction) and those with a loved one with cancer may know what I'm talking about. Every time something happens, every time there is an opportunity for something bad to go wrong, people tell you, "You will be fine."

"It will be fine."
"Everything is going to be okay."
"I'm sure it's nothing."

For Pete's sake, do NOT say those words.
After all, how do you know? What assurances do you have?

My lumps were benign until they were malignant.
My mammogram was problem-free until it wasn't.
My psyche was strong until it wasn't.
My lymph nodes were clear until they weren't.

And those blood counts and body scans will be fine until they're not.
And you do not know which is which. Even the doctors did not know for a while.

Am I supposed to go back to the people who said in a carefree manner, "It's probably nothing" and say, "I told you so!"? Is my bad news a victory against those who say in their healthy, carefree way that nothing bad will happen?

I read the following poem when I was struggling with a decision about my cancer treatment. It's short, but powerful.[*]

"You Will Be Just Fine"
Lois Tschetter Hjelmstad
(*Fine Black Lines*, Mulberry Hill Press)

Please do not trivialize
My suffering.

You who are healthy.
You whose mortality is as yet
Only dimly perceived—

Please do not say
"You will be just fine."

I may well be—someday—
But I do not know . . .
You do not know.

I love the line about healthy people's mortality being "only dimly perceived." While that is what life should be like, you are only ever a sentence away from bad news. One phone call, one blood test, one doctor's exam. This is what having a medical condition makes you understand.

January 5, 2009

* Excerpted from *Fine Black Lines: Reflections on Facing Cancer, Fear and Loneliness*, Copyright 1993, 2003 Lois Tschetter Hjelmstad. Used by permission of Mulberry Hill Press.

23

No Matter What, It Matters: The Psychological Importance of Hair

My friend Andrea found out she needs to have chemo. I cried a lot the day I found that out. Last night she emailed me that she was thinking about the whole "losing her hair" thing. She has gorgeous hair. Thick. Straight. Reddish-brown, in the sun I'd say it has a honey shine in it. She usually wears it back in a ponytail, as she says, "taking it for granted."

I started writing her back to tell her that focusing on her hair wasn't silly. There are many things about cancer that are real worries. One of them is going bald. Especially for a woman. And as I typed to her I realized the words were flowing fast and furious.

I realized all the things people had said to me when I was worried about losing my hair and all of the things people had said to me after it eventually happened.

Everyone wants to reassure you that it isn't as bad as you think it is.
Some days you convince yourself it isn't that bad.
Some days you are sure they are all lying to you.

Either way, you get through the days.

The day you take that hat or wig or scarf off and wear your newly-grown stubble or "mouse fur" out in public is a great day. (My first hair was so fine and soft and thin that it didn't resemble hair at all . . . I called it mouse fur because while it blissfully covered my head and was dark, it couldn't be cut or styled.)

So, for my friend, and for other women who are getting ready to start chemo (and those who bravely walk through the world every day without hair because of alopecia and other conditions), no matter what, it matters.

No matter what anyone says . . .
All the things they will say:
"It's only hair.
It'll grow back.
You'll look so pretty anyway."
"With a face like yours it won't matter.
We'll get you a cute wig.
We'll get great scarves.
It'll grow back in no time.
Maybe it'll be better after it grows in."

You may shed many tears over this one.
It may be harder than you thought.
I've heard some women say it was harder for them than the actual chemo.
Reports show women actually turn down the chemotherapy they need because they don't want to go bald.

It's real.
It's hard.

But hair matters.
To us,
To our kids,
To our husbands,
To our friends.

My hair has never been the same since chemo.
I'm not alone in that.
In fact,
My hair now grows "the other way" . . .
My part is on the opposite side of my head than it used to be.
I think that's kind of neat.
There's the way my hair was B.C. (before cancer)
And the way it is now.

It is a big deal.
Don't let anyone minimize it.
If they do, make them go shave their heads.
Not just clipper cut.
Straight razor shave it until there's nothing left.
Then the eyebrows.
Then the eyelashes.
And then the stuff they might not think about.
Every piece of body hair.
Of course there are jokes.
And giggles.
The Brazilian wax done for you.
It's funny.
But not so funny.

Then when your nose hairs fall out you suddenly realize how
Much you needed them.
Your nose runs constantly.
And it's embarrassing.
Mine dripped clear liquid constantly.
I was so embarrassed.
No one had told me about that part.

I had a tissue stuffed in every pocket.
Because there were no hairs to stop the drip.
Chemo drip.

You try to imagine what it will be like.
You try to picture what you will look like bald.
You pull your hair back,
Slick it back,
Try a wig on to see what it might look like.
But nothing can prepare you.
For that crappy day,
Two weeks in.
When you scratch an itch
Or touch your head
And take away a handful of hair
Or find it on your pillow.
And the sight of it is so sad,
But so disgusting
So repulsive,
That you need it gone.

And then if you need me
You will call me.
And I will come.
And I will cut it.
Or maybe I will just come and cry with you.
And remember what it felt like.

No matter what anyone says,
It isn't nothing.
It is something.

And even in the scheme of all of the things to be afraid of with cancer,
How you feel about losing your hair is real.

It matters.

And I remember.

September 12, 2009

The Changing Nature of the Parent/Child Relationship When an Adult Child Is Diagnosed with Cancer

I've invited my mother, Dr. Rita Bonchek, to write a piece for the blog. As a psychologist specializing in grief and loss I think her perspective and ability to share insights are welcome additions to the posts I make. I know that she gains comfort from talking with other parents who have children with cancer and sharing their feelings about the way that cancer has affected their roles as parents (and often as grandparents). My mother and I both hope that this piece will be an introduction to this topic. There is so much to say about changing relationships during medical crises. Perhaps today's post will allow you to raise some of these topics with a family member.

From Dr. Bonchek:

Throughout this post, I repeatedly refer to children. Even though adult in years, they are our children. When they are diagnosed with cancer, the relationship between parent and child will, by necessity, change. I would like to suggest how parents can strengthen the relationship and cope more effectively at this time.

When Lisa completed cancer treatment after her initial diagnosis (double mastectomy and chemotherapy in 2007, oophorectomy in 2008), everyone, including her doctors, believed that there was an infinitesimal chance that the cancer would return. When the cancer returned in the form of an incurable metastasis in 2012, we were all devastated.

Families have one type of relationship when all of its members are healthy and a different type when one member is ill. But cancer isn't necessarily just being ill for a period of time, recovering, and continuing on with life. Cancer can be a life and death everyday concern. So, what happens? The conversations change because references to cancer are screened, levity is uncomfortable because how can one laugh about trivial jokes when something so serious is occurring, and discussions that involve long-range planning are avoided since how long will long-range be.

Who we were as parent and child before the diagnosis of cancer is not who we are and become after the devastating news. The prior carefree mutual relationship now shifts from both of the parties interacting and sharing problems and concerns to only focusing all attention and sensitivity towards the child. There is now a one-way street. How could this not be? When one asks the question, "Whose needs are being met?" it must only be the one who lives with the cancer. The goal is, as much as possible, to reduce stress and tension between mother and child but, most importantly, within the child.

There are some tensions that occur when a parent offers to help a child with household chores, fixing meals, carrying packages, etc. A child's snappish response of "I can do it myself" may indicate that to accept the offer is to admit a weakened condition. Or, any offer to help may cause reminders that at some time, sooner or later, that help will be needed. It may be better just to do the chore without asking. It is MOST important that we do not take personally such behaviors as negativity or curtness. There can be misdirected anger at a parent instead of directed, expressed anger at the overwhelming madness-sadness of the cancer diagnosis.

It can be helpful to establish ground rules. The parent can ask, "What CAN I do for you that would be helpful?" "What should I NOT do that might be upsetting to you?"

From the day of the diagnosis, our worlds have changed irrevocably and we must adjust. I may sound as if I knew exactly what to do and employed suggestions proffered. Not so. Just ask Lisa. I let her down. I had personal problems during the time after her diagnosis of metastatic breast cancer. Lisa knew the participants well enough to understand my dilemmas and to help me. I vented and asked for her advice as she was trying so hard to just get by. Our children may no longer be as available to support us.

When I was in practice as a psychologist who specialized in grief and loss counseling, I tried to help my patients to understand, process, and deal with major losses. I often explained to them that denial was an effective coping mechanism if it allowed them to absorb the overwhelming loss little by little, bit by bit. But denial cannot be total and the reality of the situation must at some time be acknowledged. So, although I do recognize the possibilities of breakthroughs in medical science, I do not believe in nor count on miracles.

I will let my thoughts go a certain distance into the future when I must, but I function day by day as a way of living. I choose not to focus on what may occur in the future because it may not occur. What a waste of time and energy that would be. I cannot focus on the possible downturns during the treatment, on any pain or suffering Lisa could be experiencing but is not telling me about.

The reality is that though I can support and comfort her, there is nothing I can do to make her physical and emotional suffering go away. If I indulged in this negativity and worry about Lisa in my everyday life, I would have no life. I try to remember—not always successfully—that worrying benefits no one. If my worrying could provide even a tiny extension of Lisa's life, I would worry myself sick.

A line in Joyce's *Ulysses* states this emphasis on the present: "Hold to the now, the here, through which all future plunges to the past."

To derive satisfaction from life, Lisa and I agreed that auditing classes at Franklin & Marshall College would distract me with an activity that would challenge me and bring me satisfaction. And so it has. The last thing we want our children to do is to worry about us. Whatever we do for ourselves, we do for them. Find some interest or activity that gets you through each day.

Lisa and I have quite different personalities and behaviors. As her readers know, she is very open in describing her thoughts and feelings. In contrast, I was a very private person. When Lisa first started writing, I was uncomfortable seeing private information about our family being disclosed publicly and shared with people I did and did not know. But, very soon, I began to appreciate the role that Lisa's writing played and continues to play in her life and the lives of her readers. And so I changed and re-evaluated my stance on privacy. In answer to the question, "Whose needs were being met?" I substituted my privacy desire for Lisa's openness. I stand with Lisa to help cancer patients and their loved ones live with cancer and not die from cancer.

Our daughter, Lisa, is an incredible daughter, wife, mother, and friend. I cannot and will not imagine living my life without her.

From Lisa:

I think the only thing I would say that I might disagree with here is that I don't think it has to always be a one-way street. Mom refers to a time when I was helping her with problems she had in her own life. Yes, perhaps it's important to be aware of when you are asking your child for help or advice. However, if this is the way your relationship is (ours is, for example), then I believe that maintaining some of this dynamic adds to the sense of "normalcy" that may be elusive but also can be comforting to both parties. That is, if I am not in an immediate medical crisis, helping my mother with a problem she is having feels good to me, rewarding, reminiscent of the way things were before. If the street is always one way, that adds to the feelings of separateness between us, a strong reminder that everything is different.

A suggestion we both have is to focus more on parents taking care of themselves, finding ways to cope in a way that is right for them. Certainly parents and children do not always have the same strategies to deal with medical crises. The parent also may need support to deal with his/her grief during this fragile time. Individuals may find help in talking to a therapist or other supportive figure or attending a support group for parents.

There are constant ebbs and flows in the parent/child relationship based on how treatments are going, anxiety about upcoming tests or bloodwork, and the side effects of treatments. It may not always be clear how much the parent needs to be a parent at any given time. Open communication is so important. One of the hardest conversations my mother and I had recently was one in which I openly laid out some ways in which she could be more helpful to me now. That conversation led to a wonderful new phase of support. She feels good that she knows better what I need, how to be helpful to me and to my family. I cannot expect her to be a mind-reader, and the ways that I need support change with how my treatments are going. I will be undergoing treatment for the rest of my life, so it's important that we are as honest and supportive of each other as possible. I know that she has her own challenges in dealing with my diagnosis. She feels good now knowing some of the things she can do that are most helpful. I truly believe that what makes a parent feel good is to know they are a help, rather than an additional source of stress for their child during this difficult time.

June 26, 2013

Having a Bad Feeling About Having a Good Attitude

"Having a good attitude makes all the difference."

People say that to me all the time. I am sure every person who's had cancer hears that. I think what people are saying is that there is something you can control in all of this mess. There is so much you can't control, that you have no choice in. People say how you deal with it, how you choose to behave once these things are thrown your way, is up to you.

Here's what I think:

I think what matters is good health insurance. I think what matters are friends and social support to get you through. I think what matters are children, or pets, or others who nurture your soul and remind you why you are going through all of this: there are others who care about and depend on you.

I think good medicines matter. I think caring and capable oncologists matter. I think talented surgeons matter. I think getting good advice matters.

Why am I resistant to the idea that attitude matters? Not because I don't believe it. I reject this idea because it places the burden of healing on the individual patient. It places the weight of getting better in his/her hands. I think cancer patients have enough to deal with. We have enough to feel guilty about and responsible for. I think tossing our collective attitude into the mix is a lot of pressure. All eyes are on us anyway.

Now we have to watch how we treat the thing which is killing us.

Having a good attitude says:
The power is in you to survive.
The power is in you to heal.
The power is in you to do well.

But looking at the converse is troubling. The implication is that if you suffer, if you relapse, if you die—it is your fault.
If you had only had the right attitude,
you could have been better at keeping it away.

You could have been stronger.
You could have beaten it.

There is an impetus to control. You just feel like you need to do something. I think that's what people are grasping on to with their advice. They know you can't do much, so they tell you to control the one thing you can: your mindset about what is happening to you.

Sometimes I just don't want to have a good attitude.
I don't necessarily think it makes a difference.
I don't want to think positive thoughts all day
and see the good in what is happening to me.

I think that can be healthy, too.

January 27, 2011

What Does It Mean to Be a Good Listener?

How can you be a good friend to someone with cancer? Doing
the same things you do for any friend: show you care, express
interest in her life, be sympathetic, and offer to help when she
will let you. The best thing you can do is to be a good listener.

Being a good listener seems obvious, but it's harder to do than
it sounds. First, you need to remember that if you haven't had
cancer, you aren't going to really understand what your friend
is going through, what she is feeling. You might think you do,
but you don't. You can't.

The fact that you don't share the bond of cancer, though,
doesn't mean you can't be helpful, supportive, and caring. You
can be all of these by listening. Some of the most supportive
people in my life have never had cancer. It doesn't matter. They
are good friends in part because they are good listeners.

Listening does not entail giving advice.

They are two totally different acts. One requires that you listen while your friend talks. One involves you giving your opinion about how your friend can change and what she can do differently/better.

In times of active crisis, the best thing you can do is keep your opinions to yourself. Unless you truly know what that crisis feels like (the death of a child or spouse, a serious medical diagnosis, or a divorce, for example), your advice will fall into the category "things people-who-don't-understand say." For me, others' advice usually misses its mark. The result? I feel further misunderstood; therefore, I am more isolated.

My mother taught me the difference between these two acts. "Do you want me to just listen or do you want my advice?" she would ask. Sometimes I wasn't sure. Sometimes I'd ask for the advice and not follow it. The fact that she gave me the choice, asking the question directly, gave me control. I was telling her how to be helpful—what I needed from her.

I know it's not easy to just listen. But sometimes asking the specific question, "Do you want my advice or do you just want me to listen?" can help us be exactly the kind of people we want to be: better friends to those we care about.

April 1, 2009

Q&A: Ask, Listen, Respect

I get a lot of emails and comments with questions about cancer and how to help those who have it. Let me say clearly that I never think I speak for everyone with cancer. I do believe that asking questions is good, and even if you don't think my answer is right for you, at least you might look at the issue a different way and clarify your own thoughts.

This week I received the following excellent question.

Hello...

I'm a thirty-one-year-old only child whose mother was just diagnosed with squamous cell carcinoma a week ago.

I'm going home for the first time since the diagnosis and after reading this blog, I'm not sure what I should say to her. She is a pessimist by nature and already saying she would refuse chemo, so my dad and I need to figure out a way to keep her positive so she can indeed have the support she needs to fight it. I bought some colored paper and was going to list "reasons why you are a fighter" as well as post some motivational sayings/quotes on their bathroom mirrors, but the ones that came to mind now seem like the ones you SHOULDN'T say: "You can do this, stay strong."

Do you have any suggestions on what I could write? Please keep us in your prayers. I am obviously terrified of the road to come.

My response:

A few quick thoughts for you, J. I am so sorry about your mom's diagnosis.

My first thought is that you *all* need time to adjust to the news. The way you react initially is not always the way you feel once you get your feet back under you. She needs a bit of time to not only adjust to the news but also to make this treatment plan. She doesn't even know yet what will potentially be recommended for treatment and yet you are expressing desires to coach her on how to feel.

Being supportive does not necessarily mean keeping her spirits "up." Maybe what she needs right now is support for how she actually feels, not pressure to be acting a certain way. The best way to support her is to listen to her, and not try to tell her how she should feel. Let her adjust. And most importantly, respect whatever she chooses.

We love our families more than anything, but it's her choice to make how she wants to live her life and how she wants to treat her cancer. It's enough to deal with these diagnoses without feeling you are carrying the emotional burden of your loved ones on your back too. It will mean that she will know everyone rises and falls on her actions. That's a huge weight above and beyond the physical and emotional toll she will be going through.

One of the most important things to do is to **ask** her how she thinks you could help her the most. I have a feeling putting up signs is not it, especially if you say she is a pessimist by nature. Signs around the house won't change her attitude if a lifetime of experiences hasn't. Loving her, spending time with her, helping her with things that she might have trouble doing . . . those might be better. *The key is to ask, really listen, and then respect what she says.* Her needs might change (doesn't want or need help now but needs it in the future) so you have to ask again during treatment.

If she decides to refuse chemo it will be tough, but it's her choice. Chemo is very hard and is a quality of life issue too. Depending on what they are recommending and what the ultimate details of prognosis are, it's important to respect what she opts to do while still encouraging her to see the benefits (as described by her doctor).

Those of us with cancer know everyone wants us to be "strong" and "positive" but it's what we need to hear the least. It's not like we haven't thought of that already; it often just makes us feel like people are telling us how we should act because it makes it better for **them** if we act that way.

Negative emotions are normal with cancer, especially only one week after diagnosis . . . How could they not be? Not feeling free to express them may just be one more way she feels burdened by this disease right now.

Clearly you love her and want to help. The fact you are concerned with the best way to support her shows wonderful affection. The best way to do that right now, so soon after diagnosis, is to ask, and then respect what she says . . . That's my best advice right now.

She will need time, but ultimately I think that she will be grateful for being allowed to express her emotions both negative and positive. I wish you all the best. Please keep us posted.

May 24, 2013

What to Say to Someone with Cancer

At the time I was diagnosed, I was the first one of my friends to have cancer; I didn't have anyone I could ask for advice.

I was often annoyed with the comments people made. I felt some were just silly ("Well, you've been needing a vacation and now you get to lie around and read books all day. What could be better?") while other comments seemed hurtful or downright rude ("Is your cancer what is going to kill you?").

I know people come here expecting to learn. That's what I'm trying to do: educate. People inevitably vary in their responses to what people say. After all, responses to books, movies, and comedians are all over the place.

Occasionally people will get defensive and say, "Well, I have said one of those 'stupid' things and I meant well." I am going to take an unpopular stance and say that meaning well isn't always enough. It's important to remember: it's not about you. It's about the person with the illness. If you are a friend you will need to get over your discomfort or get out of the way. What you don't want is for the ill person to have to be consoling you or trying to minimize the seriousness of what they're feeling.

Types of cancer are not the same. Even subtypes of cancer are not the same. Now, I'm not saying you should always avoid interjecting something to let the other person know that you've had experience with cancer. But the first thing out of your mouth shouldn't be to connect it to someone else and what their outcome was, good *or* bad.

Different diseases cannot be compared. Different cases *of the same disease* cannot necessarily be compared, either. Chiming in with, "Oh, my second cousin's boyfriend's dog walker had breast cancer" doesn't help a person, especially if it's followed by "She suffered in pain for a long time and died" (yes, this gets said more often than you can imagine). The other end of the spectrum is, "Oh I know someone who had that. They're fine now." (Okay, but some people are not fine . . . should they be jealous? Feel inadequate?) Someone told me in response to learning I had metastatic breast cancer that his wife "had a bit of that last year."

If you had a coworker who worked the entire time she had treatment, that's great. We are happy for her, truly. But that bears no relation to how someone else can handle their surgeries, treatments, and side effects. So while you might think it's supportive (in your mind you're saying, "See, I'm being supportive and reassuring her that it might not be as bad as she thinks") what that person may reasonably hear is, "Wow, if you have to take time off work you are weak, or at least not as strong as my coworker was."

What would be something better to say to a coworker? How about, "Please tell me how I can help you during this time. Is there something at work I can do to make it easier for you? I hope you know I would like to help if I can. If you can't think of anything now, that's okay. Just let me know if/when you do. I'll ask again to make sure you're getting the help you might need."

If you want to help, you can ask, "Where's your to-do list? I'll pick something off of that," instead of saying, "Call if I can do anything." Taking children for playdates (phrased as "We'd love to have your child over, please let us/we won't take no for an answer") is a lot more likely to receive approval than "What can I do to help?"

Instead of the generic "How are you?", asking "Has this been a good week(day) or a bad week(day) for you?" seems like a good bet to ask someone you might not be best friends with. It shows concern and they can be as detailed as they want in their response.

When someone says, "My thoughts are with you" (a phrase I use often and am not about to stop) I think that is nice.

Some statements I would caution people to think twice about saying or asking: "Is it terminal?" "What's your prognosis?" "It could be worse, you know." "Everything happens for a reason." "God doesn't give you more than you can handle." "I'm sure everything is going to be okay/I'm sure it's nothing." "You will get through this."

A few weeks ago someone tweeted to me, "As a cancer survivor myself, I know that half the battle is the mindset. Be determined to defeat cancer and you will!" Then followed that one up with "I meant that if we believe we can win against it, we will."

43

Comments about someone's attitude are definite don'ts. Does that mean those who die every day are responsible for their deaths because they are weak-minded? If it were as easy to defeat cancer as mindset, people would not die of it by the thousands every day.

Similarly, comments about appearance, while rampant, can strike the wrong chord. I can't tell you how many times people find out about my stage 4 diagnosis and say, "But you LOOK just fine!" The two are not always correlated, most especially at the time of diagnosis. This is why many people don't know they have cancer and are completely taken by surprise. When people tell me, "You look great!" I know they mean something nice by it. But the rest of that comment, the dark underbelly, is "You don't look like you're dying" or in some ways more insidious, "If you look that good you can't possibly be that sick/it can't be that serious."

Don't say you know *exactly* how someone feels if you don't have evidence to back that up. *Being a compassionate person and caring friend does not require personal experience that is identical to what the person is going through.* Let me say that again, a different way: in my opinion you don't need to have had cancer to be a caring friend. It might *help* you to be a good friend if you have had cancer, but it's no guarantee. People "do" cancer differently. While the experience might have similarities, it doesn't mean we will necessarily agree on how to deal with it. Part of what I try to do here is level the playing field. I try to bring you information and advice you can use so that you will know more about helping than you did before.

Don't tell them that their science-based treatments are bunk and what they really need to be doing is just changing their diet or breathing pure oxygen to be cured of cancer. Do not tell someone who is in the middle of treatment that chemotherapy is a waste of time. You may think your suggestions of supplements/vitamins/tea are harmless, however, there are serious interactions that can dull the effectiveness of chemotherapy and other treatments. Not all lotions are good to use during radiation treatment. Not all vitamins are good additions.

One thing I think is very important is to always say to someone who is ill or has experienced a death in the family: *Do not write me a thank you note for this. Do not feel the need to answer this email. Do not feel the need to call me back.*

If you live near the person ask them, "Would it be helpful if I texted you before I run errands so that I can pick something up for you?" Texting and email help because talking on the phone is almost always too much of an ordeal and/or inconvenience. I have friends who email me at the beginning of the week to say, "I'll be at the grocery store, the drugstore, and the post office this week. Can I do anything there for you?" Some will text on the spur of the moment, "Running to Costco. Need anything?" These are invaluable offers.

If you have no knowledge of what information you are being told, admit it. People with serious illnesses do not expect you to know everything about their new diagnosis. They are probably learning a lot of information in a short period of time and may not even know the details of their diagnosis and treatment. They don't expect you to have the knowledge but you need a way to connect. I recommend when someone tells you about a diagnosis you don't know much/anything about you say, *"I don't know anything about what that diagnosis means. Would you mind telling me about it, and what it means for you?"*

How is it affecting your day-to-day life and what part of that can I help you with?

I'm so sorry to hear that.

What is the worst part of this for you and how can I help make that a bit easier for you?

If your friend is dying or has a relative who is, and they refer to the death or how difficult treatment/daily life is, don't brush it off, dismiss it, or say, "Oh, you're not going to die. You'll be fine. It will all be okay. Things will work out." Saying this to someone with stage 4 cancer comes across as dismissive of the seriousness of their diagnosis.

If the listener says, "Oh, that's depressing, let's not talk about dying," it can isolate the person who is ill, making them feel they should not be thinking about what is a very real concern or outcome.

As Julie Klam points out in her book *Friendkeeping*, acknowledging someone's wishes should be paramount. She tells the story of her mother and her mother's friend Patty who was dying of cancer. Patty wanted to give Julie's mom a pendant. Rather than gratefully accepting it, Julie's mom insisted Patty would wear it again, that she would get better. Instead, she died a few days later. Years later when recounting the story with regret, Julie's mom said, "She knew she was dying. It probably would've been comforting to her for me to acknowledge that . . . I was just afraid that she had some small glimmer of hope. I just didn't know." I would bet that if that same scenario happened again, Julie's mom would act differently.

Check in with your friend intermittently. Give her reminders that she is not forgotten even if she is not out in public. I love getting cards or texts or emails that tell me what my friends are up to. As I write this my friend Kathleen texted me to say she was eating at one of our favorite places. "I miss your company," she said. How can you not love that?

I love written notes. I save my favorites. When I'm having a bad day there is something about pulling out a card, seeing handwriting, reading a message. It's just more personal than seeing it on a screen. Of course texts and emails are great for frequent check-ins, but for a special message? Real paper can't be beat.

Other winners to me are notes that remind me of a funny experience a friend and I had, a favorite memory. Many people know I love my garden and flowers. They will send me a pretty card and tell me what they saw at the farmers market or in their own garden or what they're looking forward to about spring. Sometimes they will tell me about being on vacation and how they thought of me when they saw the water or the tropical plants and they remembered a trip I'd blogged about.

Some send a favorite poem or story or memory. I like those. I don't like religious quotations or cards that focus on people praying for me or hoping for a miracle. That assumes I am a religious person (I am not and I don't believe in miracles). I think cards should focus on the person—the connection to that person, your friendship, not what types of religious comfort or explanation the writer endorses.

One Twitter friend, Neil Shurley, wrote me a song titled "We Love You, Lisa," and then made a video with people holding up signs that say those same words. I still watch it. I always cry. It's one of my favorite things anyone has ever done for me. This, from what most people would term a stranger. Another friend, Nichole, took photographs that people sent her, combined them with poems and sayings, and turned them into a photo book for me. When I'm down it's another thing I reach for to feel support.

Does the person who is ill have children? If so, you can do what one room mom did for me this year: For school events Lizzie always asked if I felt well enough to join on any party or field trip. She offered rides to school performances. When I could not attend, she (and other moms) took photos and videos and sent them to me . . . without being asked. My friend Zerlina put together a playdate calendar and a dozen moms signed up in rotation to have Tristan over three times a week for playdates for the past six months. This was especially helpful. Sometimes I've been well enough to say we would host the playdate here. But knowing there was fun built in with his friends was a relief to me.

Finally, I always love my mother's suggestion for one of the best questions you can ask in any situation whether it be posed to a friend, a spouse, a child, a coworker. When someone comes to you with a complaint, a problem, or a rant, asking the simple question, *"Do you just want me to listen or do you want my advice?"* is a wonderful way to be supportive. Sometimes a friend just needs to cry and vent, no advice wanted. By asking you will show sensitivity to the distinction. This is what I mean by not needing to have had the same experience to be a good friend. Listening matters. It's free, and all you have to do is offer (and follow through).

And if you have a serious illness how do you respond when someone asks you how you are? If you don't want to answer in detail, one suggestion is to say, "There are good days and bad days. Today is a good/bad day." This response is also a good one after the death of a loved one. If you are having a good day it allows you to acknowledge they're not all like that. If you're having a bad day it expresses that you know they won't all be like that, either.

I think we all like to hear that we matter, that we make a difference, that we are loved. In the end, you can never go wrong by telling (or writing) someone what they mean to you, what you like about them, and what you enjoy most about being with them. This is the essence of friendship to me. Some days you need a serious chat. Some days you need a friend to be silly with. Some days you need a friend to go shopping and have a gossip session with and try to put cancer in the back seat for a few hours. There are many ways to be supportive. My dear friend Cathy texts me every morning to wish me a good day and asks, "How can I help you today?" I most certainly don't expect that every friend should do this. But boy, it means a lot that she does. I rarely need something these days. But I will someday. And when I do, I know she'll be there for me.

I have so many people in my world who care. I know how fortunate I am. I hope that some of these suggestions will be helpful. You don't need to have many things to say . . . a few good options will do.

April 5, 2013

Living with Uncertainty

I never want people to feel sorry for me—I don't feel sorry for myself. I feel lucky. I live a great life now; I've had a great life so far. I've learned a lot along the way and gotten stronger and stretched myself in ways I could not have predicted.

Cognitive behavioral therapy has been a great mental tool for me. Psychologists force affected individuals to "sit with their anxiety" until it reduces by half. In a nutshell, repeated exposures to the panic-inducing event prove to the patient that (the world will not end, they will not die, their loved one will not be harmed) if they do not give in to their compulsions.

The lesson? The body cannot exist in a heightened state of anxiety indefinitely. To cope, to survive, the level must (and therefore will) come down.

I take that insight and the examples I've seen and incorporate them into my life. I know that at each stage of my diagnosis and treatment for cancer I panicked. . . . But that seems to be a comfortable pattern for me: get new information, freak out for twenty-four hours, wake up and get to work learning, dealing, living. Taking our fears, whatever they may be, and learning how to better work through them can only help us . . . for uncertainty is a given.

October 27, 2010

Litmus Test

In the weeks before my surgery, I looked at pictures of double mastectomy patients on the Internet. I Googled "bilateral mastectomy images before and after" thinking I was doing research. I thought I was preparing myself for what was coming.

In reality I was trying to scare myself. I wanted to see if I could handle the worst; if I could, I would be ready. My reaction to those images would be my litmus test.

Some of the pictures were horrific. I sat transfixed. I looked. I sobbed. I saw scarred, bizarre, transformed bodies and couldn't believe that was going to be my body.

Days later, when I met my surgeon for my pre-op appointment he said, "From now on, don't look at pictures on the Internet. If you want to see before and after pictures, ask me—look at ones in my office. You can't look at random pictures and think that's necessarily what you are going to look like."

All I could do was duck my head in an admission of guilt. How did he know what I'd done? I realized how he knew: other women must do this. Other women must have made this mistake.

The aftermath is terrible to me though not in the ways I'd anticipated. I have no sensation in most of my chest. I never will.

A major erogenous zone has been completely taken away from me. Yes, I have new nipples constructed, but they have no feeling in them; they are completely cosmetic. The entire reconstruction looks great but I can't feel any of it. It does help me psychologically beyond measure to have had these procedures though.

Here I sit, two gel-filled silicone shells inside my body simulating the biologically feminine body parts I should have. And sometimes that thought is disturbing.

I knew that reconstructing my breasts was the right decision for me. I am overwhelmingly happy with the cosmetic appearance and the wonderful job my talented surgeon did. I will always be grateful to him for what he's done.

I definitely don't remember what my breasts looked like before. I only remember these.

I once asked my plastic surgeon to see my "before" pictures a year or two after my reconstruction was over. You know what? My "before" breasts didn't look so great.

In my mind they did though.
In my mind, everything about my life before cancer was better. But that's not the truth.

Don't take that as an endorsement of the "cancer is a gift" nonsense though.
My mind distorts the memory of my body before cancer. Then

forgets it.

My mind distorts the memory of my *life* before cancer. Then forgets it.

With time, I can get used to a new self.
It's like catching my reflection in the mirror: only lately do I recognize the person staring back at me.

For over a year the new hair threw me. It's darker than I remember it being before it fell out. It's shorter than it was before, too.

And the look in my eyes? That's different also.
I just don't recognize myself some days.

Sounds like a cliché if you haven't lived it.
But it's true.

April 15, 2009

The Decision to Have a Mastectomy

The decision to have a mastectomy is not an easy one. Many men and women with breast cancer are thankful that their cancer is in a location where the tumor and surrounding tissue can be removed. When faced with cancer the reflexive reaction may be "just get the cancer out." Statistics on recurrence and mortality rates with certain treatment options are handed over; a new language is learned, risks are assessed. How much risk is acceptable?

In my case, I needed to have one breast removed; I opted to have the other removed as well.

Let me be clear: I had no delusions that a contralateral mastectomy was going to save my life or even prevent me from having a recurrence.* I knew I could not control if my cancer would return. What I knew is that I could control how I treated my cancer, how I managed it, how I lived with it/after it. I knew there would be choices to be made. I knew cancer would not be a "once and done" thing for me. Survivorship means living with the ramifications of the disease, long after hair has grown back in.

In fact, more often than not, it's not even necessarily a reduction in breast cancer recurrence that women are after. There are other things they do not want to go through: mammograms, MRIs, biopsies, waiting for test results . . . and in my case, radiation on my left side which could cause heart damage.

I don't believe that my decision to have a double mastectomy was a guarantee that my cancer won't come back. There was much I could not control about cancer; some of that uncertainty still remains. However, how you treat your cancer, live with it, and monitor it are things you can control.

October 24, 2011

---

* A contralateral mastectomy is the removal of the "healthy" breast. In my case, the other breast actually ended up showing atypical cells that put my odds of getting cancer in that side well above normal.

Let's Go: The Double Mastectomy

I had two surgeons that day:
one just wasn't enough for the job.

The surgical oncologist would take away,
the reconstructive surgeon would begin to put back.

Before I headed off into my slumber,
I stood as one marked me with purple marker.

He drew,
he checked,
he measured.

And then a laugh,
always a laugh to break the tension:
Surgeons must initial the body part to be removed to ensure
they remove the correct one.

But what if you are removing both?

How silly to sign twice,
we agreed.

And yet he did,
initialing my breasts with his unwelcome autograph.

The edges of the yellow fabric measuring tape he used
had purple fingerprints up and down their sides;
use after use had changed their hue.

And now it was my turn to go under the knife—
a few more purple prints on the tape.

I got marked many a time by him that year.

Endless rounds of purple dots,
dashes,
and lines punctuating my body
with their strange, secret blueprint
only those wearing blue understood.

We stood in front of mirrors
making decisions in tandem
as to how my body should and would take new shape.

Two years today and counting.

Moving forward.
Sometimes crawling,
sometimes marching,
and sometimes just stopping to rest
and take note of my location.

Numb inside and out,
but determined.

Grateful, hopeful,
often melancholy.

Here comes another year
to put more distance
between it and me.

Let's go.

January 30, 2009

The Stories It Could Tell

I almost stole it: the tape measure with the purple fingerprints.

After all, my surgeon had left it in my room by accident. After he had marked me with his purple pen and left my room on his way to get ready for my surgery, he left it sitting on the counter by the sink. In my nervousness and tranquilized haze I didn't see it until after he'd left. I figured I shouldn't hold onto it as I was wheeled in ("Who knows what germs lurk in tape measures!" I thought), and that if I gave it to a nurse it might get misplaced. So I shoved it in my bag of personal belongings knowing I'd be in for an office visit shortly after surgery.

I actually forgot about it during the days I was home after my two-day hospital stay. The drugs, the pain, the shock of my breasts gone and numb chest filled with temporary tissue expanders were all I could think about.

I forgot all about it as I was shuttled around for weeks unable to drive. I wasn't living my normal life, my normal routine. I wasn't carrying my purse and keys daily. I was living in pajamas and constantly trying to adjust to a new body once the drains were removed.

Then while I was looking for my keys a few weeks after my operation I saw it: the tape measure.
The yellow fabric one with the purple fingerprints up and down its sides.
The one.
The one that had measured and determined where my body

was to be cut.
It was there in my bag.

There wasn't anything particularly special about its practical-
ity; it was just a tape measure.
Just like the ones I have sitting around with all of the odds and
ends that inhabit kitchen drawers.
But that doesn't capture the social meaning of it.
It wasn't just any tape measure. It was mine.
But it wasn't just mine, I argued with myself—it wasn't a per-
sonal memento for me.

For a moment or two I wanted it.
I needed it,
as if to remind myself what had been,
of what I had been.

It wasn't mine, I thought—it was his.
But more than that, it was theirs; it was ours . . . the other
women who had needed it.
Now I was one of them. It was a shared history we had: strang-
ers who had endured the same surgery, whose faces and names
I would not know.
We were bound together by this object which had literally
touched all of us.

And then I realized it was my responsibility to give it back.
Not for the obvious reason that it didn't belong to me.
But as usual, I thought of the other women: the ones who
didn't even know they had cancer,
the ones who were going about their normal lives that day, and
in the days ahead, only days or weeks or months from learning

the life-altering news that would change their lives.
I felt giving back the tape measure would be my way of being
bound to them, of saying, "I know what you have ahead of
you. I've come from there, and we are in it together."

And so when I went to one of my office visits, I took it out of
my bag and casually handed it to my surgeon. "You forgot this
in my room when I had my surgery," I said. He thanked me
and said, "I wondered where it had gone to."

Little did he know the journey it had taken.

April 28, 2011

Growing Pains and Psychological Stretch Marks

Growth happens in fits and spurts, not with smooth, sliding
grace.

With each phase comes
pain,
discomfort,
unease,
restlessness,
sleeplessness,
yearning.

At the time of my mastectomies the reconstructive surgeon
placed tissue expanders in my chest. These were temporary

bags of saline that would be slowly filled to stretch out my skin to make room for the silicone implants that would eventually take their place. Each week, like clockwork, I returned to my surgeon's office. He accessed a port in each expander with a needle and added saline to each side. Each time after a "fill" my chest would feel tight. The skin wasn't big enough for the volume inside, and it would react to the increased pressure by stretching. Until the skin could replicate there was achiness, tightness, a slight ripping or tearing feeling.

A similar sensation happened to me during my pregnancies. The growth happened fast; I got stretch marks. I had visible proof my skin just couldn't keep up; the growth was too rapid, too harsh, too vigorous.

I often wonder if mothers and fathers get psychological stretch marks when we are asked to accommodate changes we're not quite ready for.

What can we do? What options do we have? None. We must "go with the flow" and do the best we can. Our children grow and change whether we like it or not. We do them no favors by trying to protect them, coddle them, and keep them young.

We give them wings to fly when we give them tools to be confident
and caring
and inquisitive
and trusting
individuals.

I am often moved to tears as I watch my children grow.

I sit in wonder at the succession of infancy, childhood, and adolescence.

I know that as a mother I lack many skills, but I also know that the words I have written in my blogs and essays will one day be a gift to them too.

Not a gift to the children that they are, but instead a gift to the adults that I am raising them to be.

No matter how you measure time it always goes too fast.

The growth happens too fast.
The growing pains hurt.
The stretch marks might be invisible, but they are surely there.

December 1, 2010

The Only T-shirt I Would Wear

I'm not a t-shirt kind of girl. If you know me in real life you know I don't wear shirts with graphics on them. I don't even wear prints often. A t-shirt with a slogan on it? Well, that's just not me.

There is ONE slogan that I have seen—and a cancer one at that—that would get through my sartorial roadblocks.

I've seen this as a t-shirt phrase, and it's my favorite one yet:

Of course they're fake; the real ones tried to kill me!

I wouldn't design it like this one with the pink ribbon and goofy letters.

It would just be plain, all lowercase, very subdued. Not whimsical or cutesy.

I just may design a custom one...

February 5, 2011

Postscript to "I Think So Too"

The original post is on page 9

Sunday will be the four-year anniversary of the day I had breast reconstruction surgery after cancer. My tissue expanders were removed once chemotherapy was over and my silicone implants were put in. Last week I had my annual visit to my plastic/reconstructive surgeon and received the all-clear to now have a visit every two years. It's always gratifying when the time in between visits gets longer; I remember when I was there at least once a week during the reconstruction process.

"Did you know it's been four years since your surgery?" my surgeon asked. Immediately he chuckled, "Of course you know that," he said, realizing my mental calendar was certainly more precise than his—of course I marked the days off in my head.

Whenever I sit in a waiting room I am instantly transported to that place and time. I sit and watch patients walking in and walking out. I can tell by hearing what the time interval until their next appointment what stage of treatment they are in.

I sit in the chair, the same one I did four years ago.
It's the same chair, but I am not the same person.
My body is not the same.
There is continuity in that chair.
There is a story it tells me.

July 14, 2011

Cancer Is Not a Gift

I have a friend who says that "cancer has been her gift."
She says that it's been the best thing that's ever happened to her.

That perspective doesn't suit me. Despite being optimistic and determined, I am a realist. I see the ugly warts.

I don't think it's the best thing that's ever happened to me; in fact, I wouldn't wish it on anyone.

A gift is something you want to share.
Something you want to give to someone else.
Something you say, "Next time I need to give a special gift to show someone I care, this is what I want to give."
Cancer is not that thing.

Language matters.
The words we use to describe illness, death, and emotion are important—we should choose them carefully.

Cancer is not a gift:
It's what you get.
It's what I got.
It's a twist of fate.
A happenstance.
A piece of bad luck.

But once you've got it, you have to decide what you're going to do with it.
You can't give it away, so you might as well make the best of it.
Fortunately, some good comes with it too.
And one of the best parts is the people you will meet.

Just because you don't think it's the best thing,
or a good thing,
doesn't mean you are a negative person
or a bad person
or any particular kind of person.

In fact, it may mean you are a realistic person.

It may mean you are having a bad day.
Or a good day.
Or just a day.

And you will have those days:
Good . . . Bad
High . . . Low
Carefree . . . Despondent

Manic . . . Depressed
Terrified . . . Numb
Grateful . . . Spiteful
Bewildering . . . Confused
Overwhelmed . . . Sleepwalking
Drained . . . Energized
Proud . . . Embarrassed
And everything in between.

The days are gifts.
You can celebrate the days.
You should celebrate the days.
But don't celebrate the disease.
Don't treat it like a prize.

You are the prize.
You are doing the work.
You get the credit.

April 29, 2009

Cancer Is the Answer

Now that I am in remission my weeks are still full with doctors, managing side effects, and helping others going through
the diagnosis and treatment process. But more often than not
I'm at the computer writing. I've carved out something that
gives my life meaning apart from my family. And while my
cancer history has involved all those who know and love me, I
still think of it as *mine*. *My* cancer. Why? Because as much as

someone with cancer can try to explain what it is, what it feels like—what the cancer experience *is*—I am not sure we ever can fully succeed. Like trying to explain the love you have for a child to someone about to have their own child, you just don't *get it* until it happens to you.

And so, the cancer is mine. And that possession is providing my step to the next phase of my life. I don't wonder what I'm going to do with my time . . . I just wonder if I will have enough time to write all I want to write. If I can express for some who cannot express for themselves what this cancer experience can be.

November 21, 2010

If You Knew Suzy

Yesterday I sat transfixed reading Katherine Rosman's book *If You Knew Suzy: A Mother, A Daughter, A Reporter's Notebook* cover to cover. Katie is a columnist for *The Wall Street Journal* and went on a mission to learn about her mother after her mother died in 2005 from lung cancer.

I fear that what happened to Suzy will happen to me:
my cancer will return.
I will have to leave the ones I love.
I will go "unknown."
My children and my spouse will have to care for me.
My needs will impinge on their worlds.
The day-to-day caretaking will overshadow my life, and who I

was.

I will die before I have done all that I want to do, see all that I want to see.

I woke up in the middle of the night thinking about the book. My head spun with all of the emotions it raised in me. I think that part of the reason writing has become so important to me is precisely because I do realize that we can die at any moment. And if you don't have an author in the family who might undertake an enormous project as Katie did, where will that explanation of who you were—what you thought—come from?

Is my writing an extension of my desire to control things when cancer has taken away so much of this ability?

Is part of the reason I write an attempt to document my thoughts, my perspective for after I am gone . . . am I, in a smaller way, trying to do for myself what Katie did for her mother?

If I don't do it, who will do it for me?

And in my odd way of thinking, am I trying to save anyone the considerable effort of having to work to figure out who I was—deep down?

My original blog had the title "You'd Never Know": I am telling you things about myself, my worldview, and my life, that you would otherwise have no knowledge of. One of the things people say to me all the time is, "You'd never know to look at you that you had cancer." After hearing this comment repeatedly I realized that much of our lives are like that:

If we don't tell someone—share our feelings and experiences—are our lives the proverbial trees falling (unheard) in the forest?

What if you die without being truly understood?

Would that be a life wasted?

If you don't say things for yourself can you count on others to express them for you?

Further, can anyone really know anyone else in her entirety?

June 24, 2010

Two Cents

Don't tell me things happen for a reason.
Don't tell me there is a plan.

Don't tell me I'm supposed to learn a lesson from this.
Don't tell me I'm a better person for it.

Tell me I'm strong.
Tell me I'm tough.
Tell me I did it well.
Tell me you care.

I don't believe I was given cancer for a reason.
I don't believe there is a master plan.

I don't believe this is a test.
I don't believe you only are given what you can handle.

I know I will learn lessons.
I know I will be stronger.
I know sometimes it is too much to handle.
I know sometimes I want to give up.
I know sometimes I thought dying would be easier.

I believe the power is in me.
I believe the power is in my doctors.
I believe in the power of medical science.

I believe unless you have experienced this, you cannot know.
I believe unless you've been there, you cannot give advice.
I believe unless you've felt it, you cannot judge.

I believe in the power of friendship and love to make the journey bearable.
I believe suffering is a process.
I believe in picking myself up and pressing forward.
Again.
And again.
And again.

I believe persistence pays off.
I believe in enjoying the gifts I've been given.
I believe many people will never understand.

It might sadden me, anger me, and frustrate me.
But in the end that does not matter.
I can only be true to myself.
I must be true to myself.

September 19, 2011

Buyer Beware

Tristan got his tonsils out last week.
He got a piece of paper, double-sided.
Print so fine I needed my reading glasses.
Diagram of what the tonsils are. What they do. Where they are. What happens in surgery.
What should we expect after.
I looked at it often.

I had my ovaries removed six months ago.
I got no piece of paper.
I got no instructions.
I got no warnings.
I got no diagram.
No one told me what they were going to do to me during surgery.
What to expect after.

I didn't make the decision hastily. I didn't just ask one doctor. I asked many; after all, I have a team.

They made some guesses. They made some bland assurances. One surgeon said it would be "a walk in the park compared to what I'd been through." (Clearly only considering the physical recovery from the surgery itself.) One said vaguely but more seriously that the impact I would feel would be a "quality of life issue."

How do you quantify that?

How can you tell a woman what thrusting her body into menopause fifteen years early is going to feel like?

I can tell you.

I can tell you what it feels like for me. I can tell you and I am angry.

I am angry and the words are red and raw and fiery and blistery and nasty.

I want to yell them, twist them, turn them, punch them, scream them, mash them, grind them.

What does it feel like?

It feels like my life is over.

My quality of life is over.

It feels like the best years of my life are gone.

Cancer took a lot from me.

But indirectly, it's taken even more from me through this.

Brittle bones.

Fractured feet.

Broken ribs.

Crushing migraines.

Weight gain.

Joint pain.

Hair loss.

Skin changes. Wrinkles, skin fragility.

Higher cholesterol.

Increased chance of heart disease.

Increased cognitive impairment.

Lower cognitive functioning.

Increased chance of dementia.

Then there's the one no one wants to talk about. But you know me, I talk about anything, everything. Loss of libido. Sexual drive and sexual functioning. It goes in the crapper. Maybe it's temporary, maybe it's not. Maybe the mind can learn to overcome what the body cannot provide. I think not. But I don't know.

Here's what I do know. What do they do when they want to do something surgical to sex offenders to try to curb their sexual appetites? They remove the sources of their sexual hormones. That's what I've had done to me. Granted, I've done it to slow the spread of cancer or prevent cancer from returning. Regardless the purpose, the sexual side effect is the same.

When you remove your ovaries, you remove not only your estrogen source, you remove your testosterone source too (as well as a host of other hormones). And these are major sources of a woman's sex drive. Without these two, it's tough. Tough like chewing meat with no teeth. I feel like cardboard.

Why am I saying all of this?

Because people should know what they are getting.
Because if it happened to me, I feel sure it's happening to other people.
Because people always think when chemo is over, you are "done."
Because it's never over.
Because many of the struggles are intensely personal, private, and most people will never share.

Because some of the hardest ramifications are ones that won't just affect you. They will affect your spouse. Doctors should explain this.

They should acknowledge that they don't really know what will happen.
But they should certainly do their best to list things that they know might happen.

A decision is not a decision if you are not informed.
Informed consent is that.
I gave consent.
But looking back, I wasn't informed.

Would I have made a different decision?
Maybe not.
Probably not.

I felt my back was against the wall.
I put it there.
But everyone has a right to be informed.

Tristan's tonsillectomy is already a fleeting memory to him.
My surgery will be with me for the rest of my life.
In mind and body.

The anger?
I hope that fades.
Soon.

Unpublished

A Psychologist's Perspective on Guilt vs. Regret (With Dr. Rita Bonchek)

I've written about my decision to have my ovaries removed two years ago in order to (hopefully) decrease the likelihood that my breast cancer will recur. Though I tested negative for the BRCA-1 and BRCA-2 genes, my hormone receptor positive cancer feeds off of the hormones that my ovaries produced. To significantly reduce the amount of those hormones circulating in my body (as a pre-menopausal woman of thirty-eight) I decided to have a salpingo-oophorectomy (surgical removal of my Fallopian tubes and ovaries). I recovered from the surgery itself within two weeks; the effects of plummeting into menopause overnight have been longer lasting and in some cases, quite devastating.

As I do with almost any issue in my life, I have repeatedly talked to my mother, Dr. Rita Bonchek, about the ramifications of my decision. This angst has led to many talks about the difference between regret and guilt. As a psychologist specializing in issues of grief, loss, death, and dying for twenty years, she always has a keen ability to separate out what appear to be muddled feelings. She often has ways of explaining complicated topics in easy-to-understand terms and using real-life examples to illustrate her points. She and I have collaborated here to present some thoughts on these two emotions. The ideas on the differences between guilt and regret are hers; I have pushed her to explain things as fully as possible and helped with some of the re-writing.

We hope that they will help you think more clearly about actions in your life and the emotions you have about them.

In Dr. Rita Bonchek's words:

People use the word "guilt" more often than is appropriate. Improperly using the word "guilt" can result in unnecessary emotional distress and harsh self-criticism. The word "guilt" refers to something you did, something which you feel you shouldn't have done because it was morally or legally wrong. But what if the experience you feel guilty about was not something you caused or had control over? Then you would feel regret, not guilt.

Here is an actual situation: Ann {not her real name} was referred by her family doctor for grief counseling. She was unable to cope with her persistent feelings of guilt related to her husband's death several months prior. Bob was diagnosed with a terminal illness and he was bed-ridden. He needed constant care and attention which was mainly provided for by his wife. Bob was hospitalized for three weeks prior to his death. Ann was with him throughout that time as well.

On the day of Bob's death, his wife left the hospital room to use the bathroom. When she returned to the room, the nurse told her that Bob had died in her absence. Ann was overcome with feelings of what she termed "guilt" and punished herself for not having been with Bob at the time of his death. For months she could not function and was preoccupied with thinking how terrible she was in being absent when her husband died. She mentally punished herself for breaking the vow she had made to herself to be with him when he died. Instead of focusing on the 99% of the time she had cared for him while he was ill, she focused on the last minutes he lived.

Why shouldn't Ann feel guilty? Because she did not do anything that caused her husband's death; she was not there. If Ann had asked the nurse whether it was "safe" for her to leave for a few minutes and the nurse had cautioned her that Bob could die at any time, and then Ann chose to leave, then she could appropriately experience guilt because she ignored information indicating he could die during the time she was away. In this alternate scenario, Ann had the personal responsibility for making the decision to go, she had control of making the decision that resulted in her absence, and could therefore justly experience feelings of guilt. As a counselor, if someone warrants feeling guilty for an action, I would advise them to make a confession, offer an apology, take responsibility, and—if possible—make reparations.

By disproportionately magnifying these few minutes to overshadow all of the months of care Ann had given Bob, the result was that she could not forgive herself. After discussing the difference between regret and guilt, Ann came to see that there was, in fact, nothing to forgive. She understood that she was only responsible for her own actions; Bob didn't die because she left the room. By reframing the circumstances of Bob's death, Ann was better able to properly grieve her loss and move on afterwards.

Though Ann did not experience guilt, she did have regret, a universal experience. Regret refers to circumstances beyond one's personal control. An unidentified author defined regret as "distress over a desire unfulfilled." Regrets can pertain to decisions made concerning: education (not getting a degree), career (working at a job that offered good income but no personal satisfaction), marriage (married too young), raising children (being too permissive), medical decisions (sterilization), etc. These and other decisions can be considered mistakes.

Most often, individuals regret what they haven't done more so than what they have done. Often, people regret not taking more chances, rather than regretting the chances they actually took.

As an emotional response to a distressing experience, the sound of the word "guilt" is harsher and more of a self-reproach than the word "regret." If you say, "I feel so guilty" you should make sure that the deed and circumstances surrounding it actually warrant your feeling of guilt rather than regret.

February 7, 2011

Baby Bear's Chair

When I underwent a double mastectomy and completed chemotherapy for my breast cancer, my two oncologists and I sat down in separate meetings to discuss the always stressful: "What now?"

I had hormone-receptor positive cancer (breast cancer that is "fueled" by estrogen and/or progesterone) so I was able to take adjuvant therapy*. I opted to have my ovaries removed even though I am BRCA-1 and 2 negative.

Discussions about screenings and testing are negotiations of sorts. As the new research and guidelines indicate, doctors and patients are often at odds on how much monitoring is "just right."

I've taken a different approach in the past few years with tests not only for myself but also for my children. I always ask, "Is this really necessary? Is it important? Does it need to be done this often?" This is not to say that the test won't happen. I'm not arguing with the providers. But discussing these topics is important.

There are many factors which come into play when deciding what surgery one wants to have and what level of follow-up care is right for patients. This determination is one that a doctor and patient must come to together. Each must rely on the other to help navigate the murky waters of staying healthy.

---

* Adjuvant therapy refers to drugs taken after chemotherapy to block the effect of the hormones . . . for pre-menopausal women this would be a drug like Tamoxifen, for post-menopausal women an aromatase inhibitor like Arimidex.

I propose that one of the most important variables in this discussion has been overlooked: the psychological ability of the patient to tolerate ambiguity. That is, I believe there are some people who can live with uncertainty better than others, and the amount of uncertainty a patient can accept in his/her treatment should be an important consideration in current discussions about overtreatment of patients.

One variation that I think will help doctors and patients come to a more mutually satisfying relationship is a determination of the patient's tolerance for uncertainty. With this information, physicians can identify more pointedly which levels of acute treatment and long-term follow-up care are both psychologically acceptable to the patient and medically reasonable.

April 13, 2012

Steep in the Glory

June 18 is a significant date. It was five years ago today that I had my last chemo treatment.

Five years isn't meaningful in terms of my disease. It doesn't mean I'm "cured." My kind of breast cancer can return after seven years, or twelve, or fifteen. But it's still five years so far that I have had no evidence of a recurrence. Five years of memories. Five years that matter.

These last few weeks have been magical to me.

These were the days I fought for.

These were the days I wanted.

These are the days I longed to share with my husband and my children. And I am doing just that.

I've been overwhelmed with emotions in these weeks, seeing my children change and being so proud of not only what they do, but also who they are.

I think when it comes down to it I haven't been writing this month because I needed to hold all of this inside. I needed to let it sink in. I needed to steep in the glory that these simple days hold.

Being alive to share these days with my friends and family.

Helping others who are undergoing treatment and surgery.

My days are full and I do not take them for granted.

June 18, 2012

Inspiration: Just Doing My Job

What does it mean to "be an inspiration"? A few people have said that to me recently: I am an inspiration. At first I laugh. I guess I'm an inspiration because I'm still alive. Maybe that's enough.

What's inspirational about me? Trust me, I'm not searching for platitudes here. There's definitely more than one day's blog in this question.

I'm trying to get at "what makes someone an inspiration" and why do people think I and so many other breast cancer survivors qualify?

Is it being a mother and worrying about your children more than yourself? No. That's what every mother does.

Is it summoning strength to confront chemo when it's your greatest fear?

Is it putting a smile on your face when you are crumbling inside?

Is it speaking the words, "I have cancer" to your children, your friends, your husband, your parents, your in-laws, your brother, and all of the people in your life enough times that eventually it starts to sound normal?

Is "inspirational" when you offer to show your post-mastectomy body to women so that they will know the results just aren't as scary as they are thinking they will be?

Is it answering everything and anything people want to know? Is it putting words and feelings in black on white?

The essence of inspiration is being strong.
When you least want to be.
When you are faking it.

Strength.
When you lack it.
When you have to dig deep for it.

When your kids need dinner and you want to vomit from the chemo.
When you are too weak to climb the stairs.
And you don't think you can get through another day.
Or hour.
Or minute.
Or second.
And you just want the pain to end.
Somehow.
Some way.
Any way.
Just have it go away.
When your pride is gone.
Dignity is gone.
All of it.

Being inspirational means being tough.
It means feeling rotten but not wanting others to.
It means wanting to put others at ease with how you are doing.

It means being a lightning rod for everything bad.
A catalyst for everything good.
A spark.
A resource.
A friend.
A wife.
A lover.
A mother.
A daughter.

It means telling your parents you feel okay when you don't.
A little fib so they will go home and get some rest for the week.

Take some time off for themselves before they come back in eight days and do it all over again.
A break so they don't have to see their little girl suffer anymore.

Because six days in a row is enough.
For anyone.

Because looking good makes others feel better about how you are doing.

So you put makeup on.
And dress well.
And put a big smile on your face.
So they will think you are feeling good.

And when you switch the topic of conversation, they will go along with it—
They will believe you when you say you are feeling better.

Okay, so maybe I am inspirational. I don't call it inspirational. I can only admit to the smaller things. The micro things. Inspirational sounds big. Important. It's hard to accept that one.

But I think I'm convinced.

The reason I'm going to finally concede is that I just realized something:
That was my goal.
Except I wasn't calling it that.
I was just calling it doing it right.
I was calling it setting an example.

I was trying to show my family, especially my daughter, how you can tackle an obstacle—a big one.

I was just doing my job.

June 15, 2009

The Hidden Danger of Hope

Jim Stockdale was the highest-ranking naval officer held as a prisoner of war during Vietnam. Captive for more than seven years, tortured more than twenty times, Stockdale is an expert in how to deal with hope. Stockdale talked about his experience to James C. Collins, eventually published in the book *Good to Great*:

"I never doubted not only that I would get out, but also that I would prevail in the end and turn the experience into the defining event of my life, which, in retrospect, I would not trade."

Stockdale's next observation floored me the first time I heard it. He was asked to talk about those who did not make it home, who died in Vietnam after being taken into custody:

"They were the ones who said, 'We're going to be out by Christmas.' And Christmas would come, and Christmas would go. Then they'd say, 'We're going to be out by Easter.' And Easter would come, and Easter would go. And then Thanksgiving, and then it would be Christmas again. And they died of a broken heart."

This is a very important lesson. You must never confuse faith that you will prevail in the end—which you can never afford to lose—with the discipline to confront the most brutal facts of your current reality, whatever they might be.

Stockdale is telling us to forget the eternally positive attitude, the belief that hope is enough. He says, rather, that you must always believe you will succeed, but not place an expiration date on it. In doing so ("I'll be better by Christmas") can, in his opinion, be a recipe for disaster and self-destruction. In fact, Stockdale had a failed political career, but that doesn't matter to me. He made it through his confinement, and what he thinks about the reasons for it interest me.

I've never been a believer in the "a positive attitude is everything." That doesn't mean I don't think you generally should have one. Like Stockdale, I believe you must fight as if you will win. But, and this is key to me, you must accept that you do not know the outcome. This is where I differ with Stockdale's prescription. I believe you cannot confuse having hope with the reality that your hope may not be, and often will not be, enough.

A few weeks ago as my three children had their dental check-ups, I picked up *People* magazine. I skimmed the letters to the editor. One letter, from a woman named Barbara, referred to a prior *People* story about Ryan O'Neal having cancer. "I know that he will overcome this because he has immense strength and courage," she wrote. Barbara is not unique. I have heard this exact statement countless times.

First, I'm fascinated by Barbara's knowledge over O'Neal's outcome. To claim she knows what's going to happen to him is pretty remarkable. She has no knowledge about anything except a few quotes in a pop culture magazine and yet she "knows" he will overcome it. Second, and this is the big one: strength and courage are not enough, I'm sorry to say. Don't those who die from cancer have strength and courage? Is it their fault that they aren't surviving? Strength and courage are needed, for sure. But just having them won't do it. You can't think the cancer away.

June 28, 2012

These Things Are Not Tied with a Pink Ribbon

I hate October now. I don't even like the color pink anymore. I get cranky in the last days of September when I start seeing everything from toilet paper to staplers colored pink and sporting a pink ribbon. It's not that I don't want attention called to the disease that affects so many people including me; it's more that I think the focus has gotten misplaced.

I don't support Susan G. Komen Foundation anymore; I think they have lost their way. There is good research going on in many places, but I have come to question the line between commerce and research with Komen's support of everything from Kentucky Fried Chicken to alcoholic beverages to its own perfume while simultaneously trying to prevent anyone else from using the phrase "For the Cure." What happened to thinking we are all in this together, trying to achieve the same goals?

Last year I tried to think about awareness and what it means to me. I wrote this and it quickly became my most-read blog post. It still describes how I feel, it still expresses some of the emotions I have.

September 29, 2011

I wish I had the energy of my youth.
I wish I had the body.
I wish I had the fearlessness, the spunk, the drive.

I wish I could have a conversation with that young girl, bright-eyed and full of wonder.
I wish I could tell her what lay ahead.

I wish I could tell her to gather strength, and wisdom, and patience like a squirrel gathering acorns for the winter.
"Save those things up," I'd say, "you are going to need them . . . every last bit."
I wish I could share the perspective I've gained along with all of the love.

But I can't go back to that time,
I can't go back to that place.
I can't rewrite what's happened,
I can't do it all again.

I guess I must have done something right along the way for when it came time to fight I did,

and I did it well.
But that struggle took its toll on me and I am quite sure I will
never, ever be the same.

You tell yourself, "They're only breasts."
You say, "I don't need ovaries, I'm done having children."
But that obscures the truth.

The truth is that it does matter,
they do matter.
They say my uterus is atrophied.
It almost sounds funny when you say it.

"Who cares? What does that matter?"
It does. It does. It does.
To get rid of all hormones gives me a better chance at avoiding
a recurrence, but there is a price to be paid.
No estrogen matters more than I ever thought it could.

It feels worse than taking injections to suppress my ovaries,
worse than taking Tamoxifen. Those were easy. I had no clue
what was ahead.

I wear the skirt, I put the makeup on, I walk the walk.
But I do not feel like a woman anymore.
I'm proud of what this body has done for me:
Three beautiful children,
surviving cancer,
healing the broken bones, the infections, the autoimmune
diseases.
There is no week without migraines,
no cold winter day without icy implants.

Beneath the pretty lies ugly,
the ugly truth of cancer
and what it has taken from me.

While some may be able to go on,
move on,
forget,
I cannot.
My body will not let me.

These things are not tied with a pink ribbon.

These things last longer than a month.
This is part of awareness.

This is part of what breast cancer can do.
This is what it has done to me.

January 14, 2011

The Blog Post I Never Wanted to Write: My Cancer Is Back

Dear friends and family,
This is the last post I ever wanted to make but you all know
that I am open and honest to a fault. This week I received confirmation that my cancer has returned, now it has metastasized
to my bones. It is not bone cancer. It is breast cancer that is in
my bones. This means it's stage IV breast cancer.

This is not curable. The goal is to keep it growing slowly and keep it at bay for as long as possible. At this point how long that is is pure speculation, we need to see how it responds to drugs I will take. These could range from oral anti-hormone treatments to daily injections to IV chemo again. There are many different types of things they can try to use on this. I have already had a double mastectomy, chemo, and my ovaries removed to try to keep this from happening. Unfortunately my efforts did not work.

I will be writing more in detail about how I found out the cancer was back (be your own health advocate!) and writing along the way about what's happening and what treatment is like. My goal has always been to de-mystify this disease and its treatment as much as possible and I will continue to do that to the end. For now I am focused not on the end result but on the potential for science to provide me with treatment that will give me years of happiness with my beautiful husband and children. I do not know how many those will be.

I ask that you not ask the children too many detailed questions right now. They will be getting used to this way of life again. They know my cancer is back. They know I will be treating it. We are leaving it at that for now to let them adjust to this while we gather the necessary information.

I know I have a great family and support system with all of my friends and I already am seeing the help and love they can give. I thank you for your concern, thoughts, and wishes and you know I will be giving this everything I've got.

Please understand if I cannot respond to every message in a timely fashion. Your words mean so much to me but there are only so many hours in the day right now during this hectic time. I do read every single one though, and am buoyed by each.

Much love,
Lisa

October 3, 2012

Fear of the Unknown

I'm just not good at surprises. I guess you could call me a control freak. I'm not good at being caught off-guard; I'm turning forty this year and I don't even want a surprise party.

Sometimes I think this quality manifests itself in perceived negativity. Every so often, Clarke accuses me of focusing on the negative. I can't say I think he's wrong, I just think he's wrong about what drives the concern.

It's not that I focus on the negative. I just want to be prepared for whatever I am about to confront—good or bad. Of course, being prepared for bad things is harder. But I'm not even sure that I'm ready for good things to come my way.

Here it is in a nutshell: I have a terrible fear of being unprepared.

I never entered "suitcase parties." These type of lotteries were popular in college. A business would purchase two round-trip tickets and donate them to a sorority (or other organization) as part of a fundraiser. You packed a suitcase and went to the drawing. If they chose your name, you and a guest would leave directly from the party to go to the airport.

The twist was, you had no idea where you would be going. You packed your suitcase and showed up without knowledge of whether you were headed to the Caribbean or Vermont. It could be anything, so you had to pack accordingly.

Sound fun? Not to me. Not appealing—at all. I never entered any of them.

I was always like this. But it really changed in December of 2006. The one time I wasn't worried I got bitten on the ass. When I went back for my second mammogram I wasn't concerned—in the least. There was no lump, I had just had a clear mammogram eighteen months earlier, I was thirty-seven years old, and I had had multiple benign lumps removed throughout my life. Every time I had needed a lump removed, I had worked myself into a tizzy of fear. And each time I had been proven wrong: the lumps were benign.

So to have vague density issues in one breast a few months after I stopped nursing my third child did not provoke worry in me at all.

So when they kept taking pictures I wasn't worried. When they did the ultrasound I wasn't worried. When the technician called in the radiologist to look at the ultrasound images I wasn't worried. When they took me into a separate "discussion room" I still wasn't worried.

But then the radiologist said words that scared me . . . hearing words I wasn't prepared for was devastating.

It's as if the words she said weren't in my vocabulary. And therefore, when I heard what she was telling me . . . it's probably cancer . . . I had no reflex in place to catch me while I fell. Here I was, unprepared in every way to digest the news.

So from then on I was fixated on preparing for what lay ahead. I didn't want to be unprepared for the biopsy, for the double mastectomy, for the chemo. I walked through the world in a blur for that month while decisions were made. My body shut down and I was anxiety-laden. I knew I needed to get a plan. In getting a plan I would feel more powerful, more in control. And I did. Once my decisions were made about surgery and adjuvant therapy (chemo and long-term hormone therapies), I think I became resigned. I needed to know what to expect. I needed to know what I might be able to do to take care of my family and how to carry on during what would likely be one of the toughest physical and emotional challenges of my life.

When my hair started to come out in clumps on the morning of my second round of chemo I went to the garage with my clippers and shaved my head. I needed to take control.

"What ifs" are my lifeblood. What if my cancer comes back? What if I die from this? What if I have such a poor quality of life that it's not worth it anymore? What if I made a mistake being as aggressive as I have been?

The passage of time is helping me with these questions. I know you can't control it all. And I don't have the energy to worry all the time. But I also know that in being prepared I am self-soothing, rubbing my mental worry beads, trying to reassure myself that things will be okay.

I'm not sure I believe that yet. It's a daily struggle. But I learned my lesson by dropping my guard. As a student of life, I failed once. I won't do it again. Control what I can, be prepared for what I can't. That's as far as I am right now.

March 21, 2009

What to Do When You Get Diagnosed with Stage IV Breast Cancer: Some Starting Thoughts...Especially About Children

It's only been four days since we had an inkling from my oncologist that I had metastatic breast cancer, three days since I have known for sure. And now, in the middle of the night, it's time I long for. The Earth is spinning so fast...how can it be I've been awake for two hours? Have I spent them wisely? What else could I be doing with those days, minutes, seconds?

I've done so much already.

In the dizzying days after a metastatic cancer diagnosis there is so much emotion that it might be hard to think about what to do. You feel helpless. In some ways you are helpless until you get more information. But in the meantime here are some tips about what you can do.

I understand that not all of my readers have children. But for those of us who do, helping children adjust to this news is vital. It not only helps the children but can help relieve some associated stress for the parent.

- Don't share your news until you know for sure what your particular diagnosis is. I don't think you need to know your exact treatment; that takes time. But even knowing a general range of what might be used is helpful. If you have had cancer before, children will usually want to know if you will be doing the same thing (especially if it has to do with hair loss) or if it will be different.

- In my case I needed to have a mediastinoscopy with biopsy after my status was confirmed. It's an outpatient surgery that inserts a camera through an incision in your neck to grab some lymph nodes for biopsy. I decided to focus on that concrete event mostly . . . it's something children can wrap their heads around . . . Mom is going to the hospital (not uncommon in my household), having a small operation, will be back tomorrow night. I explained the cancer, the metastasis, and answered lots of questions, but I think the "one step at a time" was more easily tangible with the surgery as the immediate hurdle. If you will need an overnight stay for your particular surgery I think it's best not to spring that news on children if possible. An overnight absence is best with a few days' notice. Children, in my experience, are usually a bit clingy after bad news and that would provide the opportunity for follow-up questions and reassurance.

- Be sure you understand your diagnosis. Explain what words mean to children and to your friends. There are many misunderstandings about cancer and stage IV cancer. The word "terminal" might be scary. Stage IV cancer is not the same diagnosis in different diseases. Prognoses vary and some types of metastatic cancer can be slow-growing or respond well to treatment, allowing years of life.

- I think the phrase "It's not curable but it is treatable" is important to teach and use.

- Wait to share your news publicly until after you have told your children (except with a few close friends you can trust to keep the information to themselves. This determination may not be as easy as it sounds). This also gives you a day or two to begin adjusting to the news so that when you do discuss it with your children you might have emotions a little more in check.

- As soon as you tell your children, be sure to tell adults who work with your children on a regular basis. If your children have learned the news, by the time they go to school, lessons, and sports, their teachers need to know. Email coaches, teachers, school administration, guidance counselors, school psychologists, and music teachers. Grief in children is complicated and it's important that all of the adults know and can be on the lookout for odd behavior. Also, they need to be understanding if things don't seem to be running as smoothly at home or a child seems tired or preoccupied. Two-way communication is key. Adults need to know they have the opportunity to bring any problems they see to your attention easily. Encourage them to do so, whether what they observe is positive or negative.

- Use counselors, especially school psychologists. This re-source is invaluable. These individuals are part of my team. We are working together and it's so important to use them.

- I have always felt that it's important to be honest about a diagnosis; that is, open and public. I know this doesn't work for everyone. The downsides of being public about a diagnosis are outweighed by the negative pressure for children if they have to keep a secret and bury feelings about such a serious topic. Children take their lead from you. If you are up front and comfortable discussing it, your children will learn to be that way, too.

- Call your other medical professionals and tell them of your diagnosis. Not only will they want to know because they care, but there may be instances where treatments may need to be examined or medications evaluated more often. Many of the most touching and heartfelt phone calls I got were from my doctors this week. They cried with me, gave me information, offers of help, and caring. It also means if you have a situation when you need urgent medical care their office will already be aware of the situation and will likely respond more quickly to get you in to see the doctor.

- A carefully worded email is invaluable. Accurate information is documented so people don't spread rumors. Friends can refer back to it if needed without asking you. They can forward it to other individuals easily, as can you. Choose your words carefully. The words you use will be repeated so make sure the email says what you want it to say to friends and relatives.

There is so much you can't control during this time, and that's unnerving. Even taking steps like these can give you concrete tasks and a feeling of accomplishment that you are helping yourself and those you love.

October 5, 2012

Four Weeks

Sunday, October 7

My Facebook page has bloomed into a virtual garden. Friends have posted photos of their favorite flowers in a digital display of love and support. I love this idea. Each person has posted a picture more lovely than the next and I can't tell you how much I appreciate it.

I've been spending the weekend with my two older children having long talks about what's happening. Their love and concern is heartbreaking. These talks are among the hardest conversations a parent can have but are the most important. These days are setting the foundation for those to come.

I alternate between strength and falling apart, but I don't think that's anything unusual. It's still all mindboggling.

Wednesday, October 10

My meeting with my local oncologist was about an hour. The two-prong goal is to actually shrink the disease that's there and also keep it from progressing for as long as possible.

We learned that the pain I have in my shoulder and chest is actually two fractured ribs from where bones are weakened by cancer. That will not heal until the disease is reduced.

The actual plan of what I will start with will be decided Thursday, once I see what clinical trials are available.

I have disease in the fractured areas, in T12 of my spine and in a spot on my upper femur near my hip. Today I will have a brain MRI to see if there is any in my brain.

How long has the cancer been there? Hard to say. I mean, the reason you do chemo is because you figure that once cells have left the breast you might be missing some. Any cells that are left can start growing at any time. This cancer has probably been there for about six months or less.

I'm having trouble eating, pretty much confined to liquid and soft foods like yogurt. I've lost a lot of weight and know I need to get my strength up for the assault that is about to hit with treatment. I'm trying. Right now I am very weak, in body and spirit. But this will change. It must change. I'm adjusting and gaining knowledge and I had better get my head around this soon. But that is hard. I am angry and sad and scared and I go through every emotion multiple times a day. I cry at everything and nothing.

I snuggle with my children as much as I can. We do not talk about prognosis and timing, only that it's not curable and treatment won't ever end. We talk about advances in treatment and how new things are coming along every day.

I won't lie: every moment is a nightmare. There isn't a second I am not thinking about cancer now. I hate that part, how it eats my life as it consumes my bones. I know this is normal for now but I hope someday soon I can think about other things. I don't know if that's a pipe dream.

My friend Andrea sent me the most magically colored flowers yesterday. The note said, simply, "Anything is possible." I alternate between wanting, needing to believe that and thinking that might be giving myself false hope. But then I think of how much I believe in science, and drug advances, and I want to believe that's true.

As always, the disclaimer: I am presenting my interpretation of what I am being told by my doctors. It's not medical advice. It is sometimes simplification of complicated medical scenarios. I'm doing my best to distill it down but I'm not a doctor.

Thursday, October 11

Ten hours, two oncologists, two hospitals, one IV infusion of Zometa, one blood draw (during which the phlebotomist told me that "you're only given what you can handle." If I hadn't had a needle in my hand I would have punched her . . .), one knock-down drag-out fight with insurance, and the first four chemo pills taken. That was today.

My brain MRI came back clear. I found out when I was in my meeting at Sloan Kettering. Tears of relief.

After a two-hour chat with my oncologist there I made some treatment options. I will do monthly infusions of Zometa to strengthen my bones. Side effects have started already. Flu-like symptoms including bone pain, fever, joint pain, etc. should sideline me for the weekend.

My chemo regimen will start with Xeloda. Fatigue will be bad. I will not lose my hair. We will do bloodwork at one month to check my tumor markers. My ribs can't heal until the cancer is reduced. But the Zometa may help with the pain.

I will have a repeat PET scan in eight to twelve weeks. We'll see if the cancer seems to be holding steady or even shrinking.

It's mind-blowing that the rest of my life will be spent on some form of chemo. I'm coming to terms with that. It still scares the crap out of me.

But, I have a plan and I'm going to do what I can to be strong.

I'm tired and dizzy and worn out. But I do appreciate all of your messages and love. It matters.

Sunday, October 14

Sold tickets at the school carnival for two hours yesterday which was fun and normal except for the part where some people looked at me oddly or started crying when they saw me. That's hard to take. Things like "Chin up!" aren't particularly helpful nor is "Everything happens for a reason" or "You're only given what you can handle." Attitude isn't always everything. Genetics can trump all.

Please don't send me suggestions of things like ozone treatments or anything like that to cure my cancer. I'm not interested. Don't tell me about your relative or friend who died a long, painful death from this particular disease. That's not helpful, though I'm sorry they had that experience. It's not that I'm insensitive, but when you're scared, what you don't need are people telling you how bad it's gonna get. Hearing details of a death from the condition you have—I'm not ready for that yet. I know most of what's ahead. Trust me. And if I don't... just let me learn it for myself. Also, "Rah-rah! You're going to beat this! Stay strong and chin up!" doesn't do much.

I know that people don't know what to say. In most cases I know their hearts are in the right place. I don't share these quotes to shame people. I share them to educate, to help teach people comments that might be interpreted by people with cancer in a particular way.

Throughout the last five years everyone always asked me, "Why don't you just move ON?" When they said, "You're done with treatment, go live your life. We think you have a long and healthy life ahead of you," I could not. I was always vigilant with my health.

I was right. And so was my oncologist. Five years doesn't mean cured. There is a reason why I never said I was cured and THIS IS IT. I'm told I had a single-digit chance of recurrence. Statistics were not on my side. I've always been an outlier. In the negative.

This one time, though, I am doing what I can to be an outlier in the right kind of way. Let's hope this works and gives me lots of time.

As always, I appreciate the concern and offers of help I receive every day. I am loved, and I know it. I don't take it for granted.

Wednesday, October 17

Go out and find beauty in something small today: a leaf, the sky, a hug, a kind word or deed. Go do it. For me. Because you can.

(Okay, and while I'm nagging, make that healthcare appointment you have been putting off. Stay as healthy as you can. Be vigilant. #mondaypleads)

Friday, October 19

I'm doing quite well after first week of chemo.

Everywhere I've gone for medical appointments this week I have doctors telling me stories of patients of theirs who have been living with metastatic breast cancer in their bones for years (and in some cases, "years and years"). Until proven otherwise, that's the group I'm putting myself in.

Anyone who knows me knows I'm the biggest realist (and skeptic) there is. But right now I'm going full steam ahead and trying to recalibrate my life to this new normal. My body will be doing lots of work and I know I won't be able to do everything I want to. I'm already accepting help so much more than I ever have. For now I am hoping that it helps others to be able to do something practical and useful for me instead of feeling helpless . . . since I know feeling helpless is a terrible feeling when watching a friend or loved one go through a difficult time.

I won't talk about side effects today, I won't talk about negative stories today. Today is about the stories of women with this disease who are living with cancer. That's my story.

Saturday, October 27

We're in Hurricane Sandy preparation mode. I've got two re-frigerators stocked, generator propane tanks filled, porch furniture moved, flashlights galore, batteries, water, etc. I've done as much as I can to be ready and yet still I feel unprepared.

It's all about control. Loss of control is a tough one. There's been a lot of that around here lately. I try to give myself ten minutes a day where I cry and lash out at what is going on. I let it out, and then I move on. There's no other way to be in my mind. To focus on the negative only ruins the days. I need to keep reminding myself of that.

I try to do as much as I can to be "normal" . . . to do the things I usually do like some laundry and grocery shopping and go-ing to Tristan's karate class. It helps the kids to feel that things are going okay and also keeps me distracted. My motto is "I'll do as much as I can for as long as I can." That is how it's going to be.

To My Dearest Children

To my dearest children,

Someday you will understand the depth of my love for you. Perhaps it might take until you are adults, perhaps made more vivid if you are fortunate enough to have children of your own. No matter when, no matter how, I hope you will some-day learn this powerful emotion I feel for you. You give me strength. You make me fight. You give me joy. You make my heart swell with pride.

I want to see it all. I want to see every day. I want to know every phase of your lives.

You see, I am a quitter.

I know, those of you who know me are probably chuckling and saying, "Yeah, right."

It's true.

There are very few things I've finished that I have started. I think I was always afraid of not doing something well. I would start and quit . . . or just not start at all.

But let that be a lesson: there is no such thing as perfect. Try. Fail. It's okay. Take a chance. You have no idea where it might lead.

Hard work doesn't always pay off. People don't always get what they deserve. That's just the way it goes.

I didn't finish my Ph.D.

I never wrote a book.

But my darlings, let me tell you something I take pride in: you. Parenthood is a lifelong commitment. There is no backing out, changing your mind, saying "It's too much."

There is one job I'm good at and it's being your mom (I'm a pretty good wife but I do tend to nag even though it's for your dad's own good). Your flaws and your talents make my heart soar in equal measure . . . they are what make you you. You are each so different, so unbelievably deliciously divine in your own way. Never doubt that my heart bursts every time I look at each of you. I'm pouring every ounce of love into you that I can. I'm going to just keep doing it every day.

Being your mom is the best thing there is.

October 24, 2012

A Bookmarked Life

One of the defining features of childhood is innocence. As children we don't realize that things change. We think the way that things are when we go to bed at night is the way they will be in the morning. We put the bookmark in our lives and expect everything to be the same when we return to it.

Of course, as we grow we realize that's not true.
That it can't be true.
That's not how things happen.
That's not the way the world works.

And what do we say when someone still believes it? We say he is being childish.

Oftentimes I wish I could retreat to childhood. Not because of how my childhood was, but because I want to recapture that mindset, the one that says that everything is going to be alright. When people tell me "everything is going to be fine" I snort. I recoil. I don't believe them.

It's not always going to be alright.

Sometimes it is. Sometimes it isn't.

But the road you must take to figure it out might break you before you ever find out for sure.

May 13, 2011

Having a Plan Is Empowering

One of the ways I deal with uncertainty and difficulty is to plan for the things I can control. Even if it's making back-up plans for my children in case I can't pick them up on time. When I get bad news, or find out I need more testing, one thing I do is go to work aggressively getting appointments as soon as possible, keeping on top when results will be back. It's about being your own advocate. By staying on top of the process and making sure that it proceeds in a timely manner gives me a sense of control. That is reassuring, and that adds to my resilience, my ability to get through these things. I have been through it before, I can do it again.

Resilience is like a magnetic pull to life, a force that keeps me coming back for more. With grit. Determination. Heart. Hope. Resilience whispers in my ear, "You can do it. Just keep going. One foot in front of the other. It will get better. And, if it doesn't, well . . . you can take it. Bring it on."

Coping mechanisms are some of the most useful tools you can have. You will cope better if you are resilient.

March 28, 2013

And Yet, the Morning Comes

The idea for the post below came from re-reading "A Book-marked Life" (page 106). The idea that there are consistency, permanence, and predictability in the world is a mantra we simultaneously embrace and need while also knowing it's patently a falsehood . . . everything is always changing, it just depends by how much.

February 1, 2013

Each day is different. Each moment, too. It still seems surreal, this diagnosis of metastatic breast cancer.

It's strange how quickly the horrific can become regular: the chemo, the side effects, the new routines. Oncology appointments, IV infusions, medication refills all start to fill my calendar.

I start making lists of things I need to do. I prioritize them.

It's not always about what's actually the most important, it's also about finding things that bring me small moments of joy.

The small moments are the ones that bring tears to my eyes. Tristan's little voice saying, "I love you, Mama. You're the best Mama in the whole wide world" is enough to make me misty.

I still lose my temper. I still yell sometimes. Often it's misplaced anger, a manifestation of my frustration with my situation.

I haven't suddenly turned into the world's most patient person. Sometimes cancer makes me the most impatient one, in fact. I feel the clock is ticking. I don't have time for nonsense. But that's not a way to be. I will still try to be better.

I try to be the one to do things with my children as much as I can. Even if there is a babysitter in the house Tristan always reads to me at night for his homework: that is sacred. I still save artwork and photographs and remind them to brush their teeth and clean their rooms.

I try to do the little things: helping Colin with a school project, keeping Paige company while she does homework, watching a sports practice if I can. I go to the grocery store and I work on the holiday card. I still take pleasure in getting the stubborn stain out of Clarke's dress shirt that the dry cleaner couldn't.

My appreciation for my days should not be interpreted as supporting the nonsensical idea that "cancer is a gift." There is nothing positive about this disease; I would give it back if I could. I did not need cancer to show me the value of things. I always knew these things were true. I never took them for granted. I knew what demons could be lurking.

I did all I could. It was not enough to keep it at bay. But maybe, just maybe, I can keep it at bay for a while.

I still haven't fully come to terms with what this diagnosis means, but that's because there's no real way to know. We don't know enough yet. It is the uncertainty that is the most difficult part for me. Will this chemo be the one that lasts for a while? Will it fail? When? What next? How long with that one last? My body holds the answers, but it's not showing its hand yet.

I have to learn to ride this rollercoaster. I'm just not there yet. And I don't really know how long that is going to take.

I walk past people on the street and know they have no idea what is going on inside my body.

People in front of me in line at the gas station don't know there's chemo in my purse.

I look like everyone else. I have hair on my head. I ask the checkout person to pack the bags light because I can't carry anything with my left arm now (the cancer has fractured two ribs on my left side).

Sometimes I want special treatment. I want a Get Out of Jail Free card. Most of the time, however, I want to stay home. Hide out. Be invisible.

I'm still processing. Reeling. But while I'm doing that I'm living.

November 15, 2012

Memorial Day: An Open Letter to Our Troops on the Topic of Bravery

Today is Memorial Day. Each year my letter to troops stationed overseas is similar. Each year I question whether I should write something new, if it's "cheating" to say the same thing. In the end I realize that thank you never gets old, it never needs to be re-written. Thank you doesn't have an expiration date.

This year we went to buy items for the care package drive sponsored by the Darien Little League. Volunteers collect supplies including toiletries, non-perishable food, and games and send them to soldiers far from home.

My letters always have the same theme: bravery by chance or choice? I don't know if the soldiers find my musing on this distinction weird in a letter, but they must ponder the topic of bravery as often as I do.

May 27, 2013

Dear Servicemen/women,

My family and I are sending you some supplies on this Memorial Day Weekend. We want you to know that we have not forgotten you or the sacrifice you are making every day to be away from your own families and in harm's way. It's not much, but perhaps knowing you are in our hearts and minds will help.

Six years ago I was diagnosed with breast cancer. I was in remission for more than five years and now my cancer has metastasized to my bones and lymph nodes. It's not curable. As I go through treatment, people called me brave. I don't think I deserve it. "Brave" is not a word to be used about someone like me. I have gotten cancer by chance and I am dealing with it, the best I can.

But soldiers? You are brave. You have a choice—you put your lives on the line after making a conscious decision to do so. You know the danger and you do it anyway. To me, that is true bravery, true heroism.

Seeing danger and making the choice to proceed anyway is precisely how I define bravery. We all find ways to deal with the fear of death. We know the uncertainty that lies ahead. We see the bravery in others before we will see it in ourselves.

What underlies bravery: chance or choice? Can it be both?

Are we just hesitant to see the quality in ourselves? Are we just modest? Do we just act the way we need to, to get the job done?

I think when you choose to throw your hat in the ring, that choice counts for something.
That makes you brave.
That's what makes soldiers heroes.

Happy Memorial Day to you. And thank you for your continued service to our country.

Lisa Bonchek Adams

Rollercoaster Ride

It's always right when they pull the bar down over my head and jam it into my lap on the rollercoaster that I silently start screaming, "Wait! I changed my mind! Let me off!"

By then, however, it's too late.

With a jerk the car moves forward, its underbelly grabbing the hooks to lift it skyward.

By the time we are moving, climbing, the car is making a clicking sound and I am sure this was a mistake. I wedge my knees against the back of the seat in front of me to minimize my movement.

I steel myself, knowing the drop will come whether I like it or not.

And then there is that moment, that nauseating violent moment before the floating...

For a brief portion of a second I'm airborne, held in by that suffocating bar. Down we go and I slam back into the seat. I tell myself it will be over soon. I just need to ride it out. It will end.

These days I'm on a rollercoaster ride that doesn't end—well, not anywhere good, anyway.

Yesterday my tumor markers were up again, back in the range where we need to discuss changing chemo again. It's been about four and a half months on this chemo combination of Aromasin and Afinitor (I continue with monthly Xgeva injections).

This is the cycle of metastatic breast cancer: chemos inevitably fail. The cancer becomes resistant, mutates, signals a new pathway to drive its survival. We have no way to know how long each will last. When you read studies and "success" is deemed an extra two months of progression-free survival you know you're dealing with heavy realities.

And so, for now, I increase the dose. I wait. I retest again one week from now, and two. By then we'll have a plan, and likely be moving on. Another tally mark of treatments tried to buy me time.

It's too soon:

I fear the safety bar is not locked.

I fear that each time I reach the top of the hill again I'll be ejected from the ride, skyward, only to plummet to the ground.

September 13, 2013

Because I Can

I load the dishwasher, put in a load of laundry, and buy Colin a new white dress shirt
Because I can.

I walk the two blocks between the doctor's office and the drugstore on a crisp autumn day
Because I can.

I give my children an extra hug, just one more kiss, an additional "I love you" before the bus comes
Because I can.

But still I worry about today, tomorrow, and the next day.
How can I not?

I put makeup on yesterday.
I can tell it puts people at ease.
If I look "healthy" then they can relax.
If I don't look sick they won't have to worry how to act or what
to say.

They tell me, "You'd never know to look at you. You'd never
know you have cancer. You'd never know you're sick."

Some moments that's true. Some moments I feel good. Some
days, in fact. And I treasure them.

Some days it's a lie. It's not how I feel.
I know it's a compliment. I take it as such.

The phlebotomist asked me at my oncology appointment yes-
terday if I'm ready for Thanksgiving.
I wasn't sure whether to cry or laugh.
Ready?
I don't know.

Giving thanks. That's a loaded phrase.

I am grateful I have some time. I am thankful for the kindness that gets shown to me every day.
Every Facebook post, photo, comment,
I give thanks.

But cancer sucks. This diagnosis is my nightmare.

But I also know that tragedies happen to people every single day. A life can be lost without warning. I have learned of two sudden deaths of friends' loved ones this week and I see the pain those losses have caused. I learned it for myself when my mother-in-law died. She did not have time to say her goodbyes.

I don't like that my life revolves around this disease right now. I try to keep my life focused on others as much as I can. I try to check in on friends who have their own troubles. I try to keep up with the kids. I try to be a good wife and keep the house running. I wish I could be a better wife right now. I try to be strong. I try to suffer on my own time. I try at these things but don't always accomplish them.

It's an isolating predicament. Few can know the anguish, the daily trials, all of the parts of my life which don't get shared with anyone. I share some here, of course, and with friends, but much of it is my own. For now, this is how it needs to be while I continue to process and try to make sense of this new chapter.

November 21, 2012

If You Know Me

If you knew me, you would know I am resilient. Tough, even in the face of the worst news. You would know I rise to the occasion every time. I might break down before. I might break down after. Certainly after. But I will meet the challenges at each and every turn.

If you knew me you would know I smiled my way through many of my hard times. Lied and smiled and said "Fine" when many a person asked, "How are you?"

If you knew me you would know I am not a negative person. That I am not a pity-seeker, nor a martyr. You would know that I just do the best I can, and want to be dignified, and strong, but am not in denial.

If you knew me you would know I love to do things for others, more so than myself. That in this turbulent portion of my life I have done what I can to show others what they mean to me, and how much I appreciate the kindness of strangers . . . how the smallest encounters can stay with you forever.

If you knew me you would know that I tried my best to make others feel at ease with my cancer. I always tried to look "well" and take pride in looking the best I could with what I had left. I created outfits around my scarves, and learned how to draw in eyebrows so that it wouldn't be too obvious I had none. I tried to set a good example for my children, being honest with them about what was happening, loving them as much as I could, and asking the others who loved them to help them feel special and safe.

If you knew me you would know I care for others more than myself. When fellow cancer patients have asked to see what reconstruction looks like, I place my pride and embarrassment aside to honor their needs, their fears, their emotions. While some might (and do) hide their illnesses, I cannot. I have chosen for myself, and for my children, to be open about what it is, what it does, what price it demands. I believe that being this way will reduce the shame, the fear, and the confusion for them. Nothing has been more important to me than making sure my children understand what was happening and why. And scientifically what the reasons were. But that honesty is not at the expense of hope. Of optimism. Of sheer will. To remain mum about these feelings, these thoughts, these explanations of my experience is to deny my life for the past two years, to say the suffering, the confusion, the fear was ill placed. To avoid talking about the reality of the dangers, the problems, the down times is to be in denial and further, to assert that my fears are irrational.

If you knew me you would know that I write not because I wallow in darkness, or think negative thoughts all the time. If you knew me you would know I write so that the emotions can be explored, pushed, pulled, twisted, and shared in order for me to be positive, optimistic, and strong for the rest of the world to see. It is the sharing of these ideas on paper, and sometimes reaching the hoped-for connection to people who read them (whether because they resonate with you, move you, educate you, or make you thankful that you have no idea what the hell I'm talking about!) that keeps my words flowing.

If you knew me you would know I'm just a person, doing the best I can with what I've got, and with what I've been given. Maybe it's a bum rap, and maybe it is actually the greatest opportunity I've ever been given. I think it's probably a bit of both. My fervent hope is to be able to pay it forward for quite some time.

January 15, 2009

Mama Said There Would Be Days Like This

When I was growing up and there was a particularly tough day my mom would use the expression, "Mama said there'd be days like this."

Yesterday was one of those days. It was a long, exhausting day without too much to show for it in terms of relief.

It's hard not to feel defeated on some of these long days when it just seems the mountain is so big to climb. Right now we are making a change to try to get better results in controlling cancer progression. I won't be able to travel for the holidays anyway, but now I will be spending time in hospitals rather than resting at home and taking a break. Cancer doesn't give a damn about Christmas. Or families. Or anything that matters to me. But my doctors do. And they continue to show caring and concern and work so hard to try to make things better. Without that help and support this would be so much harder. Even when mistakes happen (and yesterday there were quite a few with blood draws and lab tests and so on), every doctor apologized. I definitely shed tears many times yesterday out of frustration, which doesn't happen too often.

As I waited for my results I watched the office staff exchanging gifts, talking about holiday parties and Christmas cookies. One by one they packed up their belongings and turned out the desk lights. I was the last patient left in that department. That was hard. But I also know that I got to walk out of the hospital last night. I still got to go home and sleep in my own bed. And when I got home I made it just in time to hug my children and see Tristan's artwork, all sparkly and smile-inducing. He asked me at bedtime why I couldn't go on vacation with the rest of the family again this year. I explained to him that altitude makes it harder for me to breathe. The air is thin, and I would not feel well. I asked if he understood. "Yes, but I am still sad you can't come." "Me too, honey. Me too."

I'm going to need to dig deep over the next six weeks. I'm going to need to ask for help with childcare and logistics while I'm recovering from procedures and having so many trips to Sloan-Kettering. That's not easy either. I find it very hard when I feel that I've not been strong enough, or that I've complained about the way a hard day has gone. I know it's normal to need to just cry and complain and say to the cold nighttime sky, "This isn't fair. This isn't how it is supposed to be." Sometimes you just need to vent, though.

I need to be strong for the next few days and what they will bring. I want to make the holidays joyous for my family to the degree I can. These are the tasks that make me feel like me. The family shopping is done, the teachers' gifts distributed, the tips for those who help during the year have been handed out, the holiday cards sent. These are the things that I know I could get a "pass" on. But they are the things I value. I will always try to show my gratitude to others.

Yes, Mama said there'd be days like this. But tomorrow is another day. And I don't lose hope that it will be better.

December 21, 2013

You Look Great; You'd Never Know

It's true:
you'd never know.

I look great. I look healthy. I'm not gaunt or drawn or pale.
I wear makeup most days, and some days I even wear boots
with a heel on them.

I smile, I laugh.
I take a slight jog up the front hall steps when I feel like it.
I crack jokes, I roll my eyes when standing in a long line, I
gossip with my friends.

I wear gloves a lot, I have to moisturize my feet and hands at
least a dozen times a day.
I buff my feet, I examine them for cracks and bleeding. I stick
ice packs on them when they burn from the chemo.
I can't feel my fingertips, yet portions of them crack and peel
and are painful and raw.
I can't hold a pen or twist off a bottle cap.

I take pills all day long.
I'm swollen, I'm tired, my mind can't stop racing.

I tell time by "on" weeks and "off" ones.
Of course the doctors understand my situation.
They know what this diagnosis means.
Even ones that have nothing to do with cancer call to check on me.

When I go to my sons' school some of the teachers and moms cry when they see me.
"You look good," they say. This is a compliment. Sometimes they say, "You don't look sick at all. You'd never know."
That is shorthand for, "You don't look like you're dying but we know you are."

I hear people in line to buy holiday gifts complain about the sniffly cold they have or the poor night's sleep their child had.
They might be complaining about something more serious, but still something that can be fixed.
Time will heal what ails them.
I am not so lucky.

I am jealous.
I am jealous that this is their only medical concern.
I'm not jealous of what they wear or the car they drive or the house they live in.
I'm jealous of their health status.

I'm not in denial. This diagnosis is a nightmare.
My life will always be full of chemo and side effects and worry and monitoring and drug refills and hospital visits.
But my life will also be full of great memories, of laughter,

of smiles.
There will be tears. There will be pain. There will be heartache.
But there will also be joy, and grace, and friendship.

I don't know for how long. I don't know if they will be in equal
measure.
They say I look good. They say, "You'd never know."
For now I know it's true.

There will come a day when it's not true.
And they will lie.
And I will know it.
And someday, then, I will know the end is near.
But that day is not today.

December 30, 2012

So Much Left to Do

There's salt on my blue jeans
And rain left in my hair.
There is a spot of dirt behind his left ear
And mud on his shoes.

I don't wipe the spot of dirt off.
I stare at it throughout the drive.
I think of when he was a baby, a toddler, a boy.
Now he approaches manhood,
A time when most young men would pull away.

He does not.
He still hugs me in public.
He tells me he loves me.
He doesn't mind if anyone hears me tell him the same.

He is still mine for a little while longer.

As I contemplate the dirty spot,
I hear the words.
They write themselves
As they often do.

The salt, the dirt, the refrain.

"There is so much left to do."

It is a track stuck on repeat.
Every moment of my life now it plays.

I showed him a better hamburger today,
He will remember that.
I reminded him about bringing dry socks to the game.
I am quite sure he will forget about that.

I can't help but smile every time he looks my way.
Or waves from the mound.

During the delay he caught rain in a water bottle,
Shrugged his shoulders when I caught his eye.
He beamed his impish grin.

Later he asks me, "Do you need help?"
He thanks me for coming to his game.
He knows.

The salt is gone from my jeans.
The rain in my hair has long since dried.
The dirt and mud are gone too.
But there is so much left to do.

October 7, 2014

Chicks in the Nest

A reader asked in the blog post "Open Season" about the fear of dying before your kids are ready to be "launched." For the purposes of this piece, I'm going to assume "anonymous" is a woman. The pronoun thing gets too distracting otherwise.

She's tapped precisely into the locus of the fear.

It's not about dying—the dying process—for me. Neither is it about what happens after.

It's about leaving your loved ones behind. It's about leaving the little ones, the fragile ones, the ones who can't yet fly. There's always something you'll want to ensure for the fragile. Something you'll want to make sure is set for them.

If the fragile one is a parent, you'll want to ensure they are safe and taken care of. If it's a child with special needs, you'll want to ensure they have the right caretakers, therapists, home care. For children there will always be something you will want to see: a milestone, a graduation, a wedding, a grandchild. First prom, first date, first kiss, first love letter, first day of college. Life's little moments.

The moments that add up to make a lifetime.

But there is another person you fear leaving behind: your spouse. This is tied in to your fledgling chicks and their future. One of the things you can do to ensure their growth and development is to get your friends involved. Friends you trust. Friends who are good parents. Just because a friend may be a great friend to you doesn't mean they would be great "bonus" parents for your children.

I am lucky to have a friend who is not only a great friend to me, but is a wonderful mother. The best mother. She raises her children the way that I want mine raised. When I was going through chemo I pestered her. I pestered her that if I died (of course you always use the "if something happens to me" phrase) I wanted her to watch over my kids, and watch over my husband. I wanted her to make sure he chose someone that was "right" for my family. I knew that her radar was the right radar, that she would know what was right for them. This was a way that I could have some sense of calm, some sense of knowing that a cuckoo would not come and steal my chicks in my absence. (I love that it's the cuckoo bird that comes and steals other birds' chicks. It makes a perfect metaphor for the "wrong" kind of person who might come into my family!)

You can't get around the fear of leaving your family behind. It's real, it's part of being a mother. It is the hardest part, because it's the lioness part of us. We fear for others more than we fear for ourselves. Death is hardest not on us, but on those we leave behind. All we can do is be honest, and prepare our loved ones.

It is a constant process, though. It is like tending a garden. I am constantly explaining, and re-explaining. As our children grow, their capacity for understanding grows and changes. You can't explain death, or cancer, or illness once and expect that to suffice.

Children forget. Children fill in the blanks. They often fill the blanks in with inaccuracies. It's the job of the cancer mom to bring them back on track and re-educate them as they get older and they can understand more. I explain any new treatments to them and what I have ahead of me. If they understand what I am going through they will learn to be sympathetic and caring children (and therefore adults).

The world needs more of those.
That I know.

June 8, 2009

Alone

I wrote this because it strikes at the core of what I feel so often. Sometimes feelings like loneliness can be the hardest to describe.

I can see how isolating metastatic cancer can be already. (I know these feelings are not unique to cancer.)

It has become hard for me to be around other people.
I find myself hiding as much as possible.

When I am in the company of others my mind wanders.
I can't focus. I feel the need to retreat.
For the time being I just can't relate to others' lives which only six weeks ago were so similar to my own. Now . . . we are a world apart.

It's not their fault. It's just that circumstances make it so that I am selfish. I try to conserve my energy as much as I can.

Already I can see relationships suffering. There is a fine line between giving space and putting distance. Some are already dropping away, and we've only just begun. Others have risen to the occasion and helped more than I could have dreamed. Only true friendships are going to make it under these circumstances. Sometimes the isolation comes from being shut out. Sometimes it comes from locking yourself away.

Phone calls go unanswered, emails often do too. Thank you notes don't always get written, social commitments get canceled or never scheduled in the first place.

I know that people cannot truly understand.

I don't want a support group right now because metastatic cancer has a wide range of outcomes. I don't know if I will be in a rapidly progressing group or not. I don't know whom to look to that is "like me." There is no way to know which group I will be in, who my peers are.
Right now I am very sensitive to death, to pain, to suffering. I'm too raw. I just don't think I'm ready for a group. But I won't say I never will be. I need to talk to my oncologists about whether they have patients like me.

It's difficult to listen to people complain about trivial things, normal things, things I was complaining about two months ago.

Now those complaints just annoy me, or make me sad.

I want to scream, "I want your problems!" And I do. I want that life back. I want to turn back the clock. I just don't want it to be this right now.

One of the things that bothers me the most about this disease is the knowledge that the way I feel right now is the best I will ever feel for the rest of my life. It's only going to get worse. That thought terrifies me.

When you feel crappy you want the time to go faster. You just want to get through it.

The problem is that what you may not have is time.

It's a conundrum. You want the time to pass, but this is the only time you have.

I know so many people say, "No one ever knows how much time they have. You have to make the most of every day, of every moment." I know that's true. But the knowledge that there is something identifiable in your body that is a threat, is most likely to be that which kills you, bears a different weight. Of course the doctors don't know exactly how much time it will be. There is no crystal ball.

Everyone tells me the stories of friends and relatives who were told they only had months, and years later they are still alive and doing okay. I am told these stories every single day. I get it. I do. And I love them; they give me hope. But often those people's diagnoses and particulars bear no relation to mine.

Additionally, there are also stories of the people in the other group, the ones who thought they had years and didn't. People probably have the good sense not to tell me those stories. But they are out there. It's not that I focus on the negative. It's not that I necessarily think I will be in that group. But anything is possible. On both sides.

The part that scares me: I'm only at the beginning. I hope that I will get stronger, gain acceptance as I get used to this diagnosis. But I'm not sure about that. I truly believe I could handle this better if I didn't have so much worry about my children and what effect this will have on them. I wish I could protect them, shield them from this agony.

There are good days and bad days. I must do my best. But being the one everyone is watching takes a toll. Everyone will take their cues from me. I will set the stage for how my friends and family will deal with this: how I handle metastatic cancer matters. I am laying groundwork. I must do it right.

Some days that is an overwhelming task.

"Doing it right" doesn't mean I have to be positive all the time. Doing it right means I have to be honest. It means I get up each day and do the best I can. For myself, for my husband, for my children, for others who may have cancer and those who will get it. It's okay to be scared, and angry, and sad, and everything else.

It's all part of this.
And for me, so is sharing.

November 24, 2012

The Passenger

A thermos of tomato soup sits in the cup holder.

Trees become a blur outside my window as we make our way across the Pike from Boston.

I take note of the wispy clouds in the azure sky.

Usually I can't truly appreciate the view because I am in the driver's seat, focusing on the cars in front of me.

This Thanksgiving I am in the passenger seat.

I am the one handing items to our three children in the back.

I've given up a few things I am not so good at right now, things that take too much energy or cause pain.

I wear big sunglasses to shield me from the bright glare.

More than once on this trip they've hidden hot tears when a gentle song comes on the radio about love and missing some-one you care about.

We talk about next year.

We talk about the trip we'll make to see family again.

I nod, I say, "Of course."

I do not protest.

But the voice inside my head wonders if they are pipe dreams, if I will actually be able to do that.

Cancer is in the driver's seat on this trip.

But I hope it won't be for long.

December 3, 2012

Nightmares of One Kind or Another

I wake up in the middle of the night with a start:
Heart racing, breathing fast.
It was a dream, I soon realize. What I fear is not true.
The despair, the nightmare, the horror.

All of it was a creation of my mind.
In the dream I was searching for him.

He was gone.
He just disappeared.
My child jogged off into the woods, his identifiable gait
Seen from behind,
Tennis whites lit up the woods—
But where was his racquet?
I realize now in the dream he didn't have it.
He ran off never to be seen again.
Did not get to his destination.
I searched. I could not find him.

I failed him.
I quickly erase the fiction from my mind,
It's not true I tell myself:

It's a dream.
Focus on something else.

It's 12:56 AM.
My heart settles back to its rhythm
I hear the rain,
My children are safe in their beds.
I can relax now.

But ease does not come.
My fear is misplaced.
The nightmare still persists.
The reality is a different image.
There is a nightmare.
A waking one.

One that's real and true, one I cannot shake off with time, or
more sleep, or distraction.

My nightmare is loss, it is my children out of my grasp, it is
separation.
I still fear all of those things.
But it is I who will wander off into the unknown
Leaving others behind
Waking in the middle of the night with only an image of me,
Fleeting,
As they search for me in vain.

I will be there, with them, but only in memories.

It will have to be enough.
But I know it won't be.
After all,

This is what cancer nightmares are made of.
This is what grief does.

I cannot do more, be more, than I am right now.
But I can want more.
It is a parent's prerogative.
I am greedy.

I make no apologies for wanting to see the things I want to see,
Wanting to share the things I want to share,
Wanting to live the life I want to live.

This is what I want.
This is what I hope.
This is what I dream.

December 10, 2012

Decisions

Tuesday's visit with my oncologist at Sloan Kettering was informative, as always. However, the big question can't be answered: what is the trajectory of my stage IV cancer?

There will be no answer to that for now.

We start with a chemo. We see (through bloodwork and PET scans) how the cancer responds. If it responds, I stay the course until the treatment stops working or the side effects become untenable or dangerous. There is no way to know how long that will be.

Any particular chemo could be ineffective from the get-go. It could fail after months. It could fail after years. Then you go to the list of options and decide on a next chemo regimen.

This decision is not always easy; you can't know which one will be best for you. It is often educated guesswork at best. There can be many chemotherapy options and in the end, I will probably try many/all as each one eventually fails.

When a doctor is hesitant about a treatment I always advise people to make sure to ask, "From a scientific point of view why do you discourage me from pursuing this and what other option do you think is better and why?" The option may be to do nothing but that also should be justified with a scientific/ medical rationale. All patients deserve that.

I've talked to women who have gone through more than eight different chemos in the treatment of their metastases. One thing I know is that chemotherapy in one form or another will be a part of my life for the rest of my life.

There is also no way to know if you will tolerate a chemo regimen well. Side effects can be dangerous and variable. Sometimes side effects are serious enough that you must discontinue using a particular drug even if it's effective in reducing the cancer. As you can imagine, this can be a heartbreaking proposition: find something that works but you are unable to take.

I continue to do as much as I can every day and when people see me and say, "You'd never know what you're going through right now," I take it as a compliment. I was busy today with routine dentist and endocrinology appointments . . . you can't ignore the rest of your body when you are treating cancer. Many other body systems will be affected by the cancer and chemo.

It's important to keep a watchful eye on your whole body and not use cancer as an excuse for ignoring routine checkups. That's my loving nag for the day . . . stay vigilant with your healthcare appointments and thanks for all of your support.

December 12, 2012

Six Years Later: It's Not a Miracle, It's Chemotherapy

Today marks the six-year anniversary of the day I was first told I had breast cancer. When the radiologist told me the news, she also said she didn't know exactly what it was or how bad it was.

This is why you do not schedule mammograms or biopsies right before a holiday. Especially Christmas. You'll be going on vacation . . . and if you aren't going on vacation, the doctors, nurses, and pathologists will.

I was told on December 20, 2006, that I almost certainly had cancer based on the mammogram and ultrasound images.

Almost six years later, I have now found out that I have stage IV (metastatic) breast cancer.

The concept of "good news" has been completely redefined since my new diagnosis. There is no cure, so I can't hope for that. There is never going to be a day I am not aware of running out of time. Now "good news" gets defined as stable disease. If you're lucky, and the chemo is working, good news can even mean reduced disease. Now I hope for that.

I look at my oncologist's face when he walks in the room. I scan it for signs of what kind of news day this will be. The day he told me about my metastasis I read his face. When he walked in that day I asked him how he was and he said, "Not good." I assumed it was something about him, his family. I immediately starting worrying about the bad news he was going to tell me about someone else. But it was my bad news. It was my nightmare.

I never used the word cured. I never said it. And I don't like when others do with my kind of cancer. I always prefer the technical terms NED (no evidence of disease) which means it may be there, but we can't detect it with the tests we have done. I don't even like the term "cancer-free" for my particular cancer . . . again, there might be cancer there, but just not enough to be detected or can't be with the tools used.

Five years had come and came and gone. Even nurses in other specialties would say at my checkups, "Oh! Five years! That means you're cured!" and when I'd explain to them that it actually didn't mean that at all with my kind of breast cancer they would look at me quizzically.

"SEE?! I told you!" I want to go back to say to all of them. I was vigilant for a reason. It "shouldn't" have happened based on the statistics, the predictions. But it did. And now the only life I've got is spent dealing with it.

I watched my oncologist's face yesterday. We've had some bloodwork results in the last two months that have been a good first step but he hasn't been willing to budge much on declaring that this chemo is working. One or two data points are not enough for either of us to feel confident, actually. But yesterday we got our fifth data point.

I still have metastatic cancer. That isn't going to change.

But I have some news I can finally share: my bloodwork is showing "indisputably" (in the words of my doctor) that my cancer is shrinking. The chemo is working. The pills I've been swallowing, seven or eight a day for seven straight days at a time, in alternate weeks, are doing what we'd hoped. The cancer is still there. But it's smaller. But it's responding. It's been consistently trending down since I started on Xeloda. Now, with more than a few data points, we can finally characterize the effect and I can share it publicly.

So what does that mean? I know that's the question most will ask. It simply means this is the chemo I stay on for now. It means that I just keep doing what I am doing. I'm not "cured" or "feeling better" or "cancer-free."

It means that modern science and pharmaceuticals are giving me some time. For today, the cancer is responding, shrinking. And in the land of stage IV cancer, that's unmitigated good news. Make no mistake, it's no Christmas miracle. It's not happening for any other reason than the fact that I am aggressively taking as strong a dose of this drug as I can tolerate, and it's doing its thing.

Six years ago I went on Christmas vacation and feared for my life. I was scared and confused and miserable. Now, six years later I'm in a much worse place vis-a-vis cancer but my mind-set is different.

I'm coming to terms with accepting the life I have—the one I thought I'd have is gone. I have created a new one. The best one I can.

For today, I celebrate the good news. I will go to my children's school holiday parties. I will smile. I will make memories. I will not focus on side effects. I will find beauty in something small.

I will savor the things I can do today.

December 20, 2012

Sometimes

Sometimes doing everything you can is not enough.
Sometimes your best isn't good enough.
Sometimes things don't work out the way you want.
Sometimes it just isn't fair.

Sometimes the end comes too fast.
Sometimes time won't slow down.
Sometimes your plans won't happen.
Sometimes those dreams won't come true.

Sometimes your life feels like a nightmare.
Sometimes nightmares happen in the day.
Sometimes uncertainty is a needy child that won't leave your side.
Sometimes there isn't enough strength.

Sometimes it's more than you can handle.
Sometimes the end is near.
Sometimes there isn't anything you can do.
Sometimes staying strong isn't an option.

Sometimes a word or gesture or deed can bring you to tears.
Sometimes strangers show the kindness that should be shown by friends.
Sometimes you can't see which way the road will go.
Sometimes all you can do is research, then close your eyes and guess.

Sometimes strength may look like denial;
Sometimes you must trick yourself to get through the day, or hour, or minute.
Sometimes the reality is so unfathomable you must push it aside.
Sometimes the pain is too great.

Sometimes people don't understand.
Sometimes they make what's hard even harder.
Sometimes the kindness of friends makes things bearable though,
Somehow the strength of love can keep you going for a while.

Sometimes you get lucky.
Sometimes you don't.

Sometimes what happens has nothing to do with you.
But somewhere, deep in the darkness, you must hold out hope.

December 27, 2012

Stopping and Starting

I realized it's time for an update . . . but confess I've started and stopped this one a few times. Somehow when things are going along somewhat easily it's easy to do the updates. This is the first one I've had to discuss side effects and I hesitated a lot about what to write and whether to post it. I wasn't sure about talking about these things lest they be seen as complaining. My goal has always been to educate and inform above all.

Friends on Twitter assured me that talking about the daily in and out of chemo treatment for metastatic cancer is important. Not only are they learning what it's like, but it tells people what I'm dealing with and what activities might be hard for me on a daily basis. One Twitter follower also said that for those who have family members with this disease and might not be forthcoming with detailed information, some of these updates give them an idea of what it might be like for their loved ones. While treatments and surgeries vary so much, I thought this was an excellent point.

So . . . I've opted to continue to share these things. It's the reality of cancer. It's the reality of *MY* cancer.

I'm struggling at the moment with Palmar/Plantar Erythro-dysesthesia or Hand/Foot Syndrome (HFS). This is a common side effect of Xeloda, the chemo I am currently taking. In short, the capillaries in the hands and feet rupture and the chemotherapy spills into the extremities. Redness, swelling, burning, peeling, tenderness, numbness, and tingling can accompany it. While it does not always start right away, once you've had a few rounds it's likely to be a cumulative effect.

Driving was one of the hardest things yesterday, the pressure from the steering wheel (or anything against my hands) was difficult to tolerate. I wear cushiony gloves most of the day now and follow all of the guidelines to keep it at a minimum. My hands are more sore and sensitive than my feet this week but not as red as my feet. Thankfully while I could not hold a pen during most of the day, I could still do some typing. A long-term side effect of this particular drug is the potential to lose your fingerprints. I see an episode of CSI coming on that one!

I'm still doing everything I can and am out and about as much as possible. I still bring the kids to the bus in the morning and try to do errands like the grocery shopping as often as I can. I ask for help with things that really are tough on my hands like stuffing the holiday cards or doing laundry or dishes. Even small tasks give me a sense of accomplishment and normalcy so while the weather holds I continue to do them. Once ice and snow set in and my concerns about slips and falls and bone breakage rise I will get help with more of the outdoor things.

December 8, 2012

The Hard Truth

I'm constantly haunted and angered by the language we use with cancer. I woke up in the middle of the night last night and this is what was in my head. I feel the need to caution: please don't over-interpret this post; my health status has not changed. I'm not stopping chemo or any such thing. I've had a few acquaintances die of cancer this month and that's where this is coming from.

People die of cancer every day.

Do you think they didn't try hard?
Keep their chins up?
Think positive?
Stay strong?
Do their best?

They did.
But it wasn't enough.
There is no consolation.
Sometimes there is no "getting better" or
"Kicking cancer's ass."
Sometimes there isn't anything else to do but accept the finality.

That's not giving up,
That's accepting what is.

January 3, 2013

Reading Cues

When you have cancer you become an expert in reading cues.

Actually, when you're in any serious situation I think that's the case.

So when the nurse showed me into my oncologist's office this morning, instead of to the usual exam room, I didn't even make it through the doorway before forcing him to look at me while I said, "Uh-oh. This is not good."

The door closed and he turned the computer screen to me. "Well, it's not awful. It's not terrible, but it's a change."

We looked at the trend of my tumor marker tests since October when I was diagnosed with metastatic (stage IV) cancer. Since that time my markers have declined quite consistently (with one exception which I'll explain in a bit).

I get my blood drawn every two weeks. Some oncologists might think it should only be done monthly at this point. But my doctors and I are data people. Hey, when the news is good, who doesn't want to hear/see it as often as possible? When it's bad news, I could use it less frequently, thank you very much.

This week's tumor marker was elevated slightly over the one from two weeks ago. It's almost exactly what it was one month ago. The fact of the matter is had we drawn it monthly we'd be saying it's stable.

But seeing this one blip now causes conjecture and concern. For now, it's just a blip. We don't know if it's an anomaly or part of a trend. There's nothing to do but stay the course and wait.

My hands have been worse this round. My oncologist warns me that most people can't tolerate long-term use of this drug. I am not thinking about that. I'm thinking about bearing whatever I can for as long as I can if it's working. The question is now: is it still working?

My feet are doing well actually (strange to be posting a "foot update" but...). They are very sensitive to shoes so I wear furry slippers at home and at least now that it's winter I can wear soft-lined shoes during the day. I do not have significant pain while walking. That is great in terms of quality of life.

My fingertips are simultaneously numb and very sensitive at the very tips. They are peeling and any pressure hurts. The finger wrinkles where the actual fingers bend (to grip) are white and cracked and sore. But I am able to drive which is a real help.

My shoulder (from the fracture in the collarbone area) is feeling much better. I still don't lift anything on that side but day-to-day it doesn't cause me discomfort like it did. This is good; it means the bone is healing as the cancer shrinks it and the bone strengthener that I take by IV is helping.

After we see what the bloodwork shows in two weeks we'll re-evaluate everything. It might be time for the PET scan, might be time to try a higher dose again of this chemo, might be time to watch and wait a bit more (it would be too soon to abandon ship on this chemo with just two data points).

I'll discuss all of these issues with my other oncologist next week and I'll count the days, minutes, and seconds until I get my next results back.

January 15, 2013

Waiting. Again.

They say that bad news is easier to deal with than uncertainty. I do believe it's true. Give me something to deal with and eventually I figure out how to cope with it. I still am figuring out how to cope with a diagnosis of stage IV breast cancer. That one may take me the rest of my life. In that way, I hope it takes me a long time to figure it out.

The evil of "waiting" is a popular topic among those with illnesses. We spend an awful lot of time waiting. We have copious amounts of time in waiting rooms, exam rooms, lab offices, hospital admissions, chemo rooms and on and on. Then there's the other kind of waiting: test results, scan results, waiting to see if treatment is working, time elapsed to see if abnormal test results are a fluke.

I'm in one of those waiting periods right now. My blood test this week showed an increase in tumor markers. This usually signifies that chemo is not working well anymore and the amount of cancer is increasing. However, as I've discussed many times before, this test is not precise. There is a reason it isn't a screening tool to see if someone has breast cancer. It's not a great test, but it's one of the only ones we have. I'm not going to mention particular numbers here because the variation among individuals is so great and interpretation of trends over time is important and I don't want anyone to be comparing their numbers to mine without a doctor's help.

The jump in number was more than what can just be dismissed as normal fluctuation. But one blip does not a chemo failure make. A few months ago I had a few rises over the course of six weeks before my oncologists decided this was picking up resistance to chemo even before my scans showed any change. We try to keep ahead of it. My choice to monitor often and closely is not the right choice for everyone. Not all doctors would even agree to such a schedule. Each person finds the balance of time and testing that works for them.

So, for now I wait. We recheck, see what the data points are. One anomaly won't be reason for an immediate change in treatment with my team. I've been through this once before, watching slow rises and then needing to change chemo. I didn't think it would come again this soon. I'm hoping it hasn't.

I hope for the best, I prepare for the worst. That's all I can do.

But the waiting? The waiting is a nightmare. But I do always recognize that in that wait there is hope, because waiting is time.

If hoping and wishing could make things so I'd be cancer-free, or at least with chemo working for decades.

If wanting something could make it so . . .

Oh . . . there's a long list for me on that one.

July 19, 2013

The Tortoise and the Hair

I wish I had been more accepting of help in the early days
when I was first diagnosed with breast cancer in 2006. I wish I
had not seen it as a personal "weakness" the way that I express
in this piece. I don't want to change what I wrote then, but I
do want to say that I don't think I was right to push myself
so hard. If I had it to do over again I would accept help more
often—maybe not for the hair-washing, but definitely for other
tasks that I should have outsourced. I have learned from my
experience and I now try to graciously accept help when it is
needed.

One of my favorite romantic movie moments occurs between
Denys (Robert Redford) and Karen (Meryl Streep) in the
movie *Out of Africa*. The two lovers are out in the African des-
ert at a fireside camp. Karen leans her head back into Denys's
hands. He washes her hair gently, then cradles her head in one
hand and pours water from a pitcher, slowly and gently rinsing
the soap from her hair after he's done washing it. It's a tender
moment, to me utterly soft and sensual.

Before I left the hospital after I had a double mastectomy, the
staff told me I might not be able to lift my arms over my head.

With both sides affected, they said I'd likely be unable to wash my own hair.

Recovery is slow in the week after surgery. A clear thin tube (like aquarium tubing) is literally sewn into a small hole in the skin under each arm. It carries excess fluid away from the mastectomy site as it heals. Fluid is collected into a small "bulb" and measured every few hours. After certain medical criteria are met, the drains are removed, the incisions sewn up, and then you can finally take that longed-for shower. Eight days after the surgery I received the all-clear. As any mastectomy patient will tell you, the day you get your drain(s) out is a great day.

Only then did I try to lift my arms. And hurt it did. I tried to shrink down into my body. I tried to be a tortoise withdrawing my head back inside my shell, shortening my height so I wouldn't have to lift my hands so high to reach my hair. It was a painful challenge. I worked up a sweat trying to get my fingers to touch my scalp. I knew it was a questionable proposition. But I thought I could do it.

I thought about that scene—that romantic, tender scene from *Out of Africa*. And I started laughing. I laughed and I laughed and tears came down my face. That cry hurt. It was one of those "I'm laughing and I'm crying and I'm not sure if it's funny or sad or both and I don't want to think about it so I'll just go with it and I hope I'm not on *Candid Camera* right now . . ."

I was laughing at the absurdity of it. Here I was. It was my chance to get Clarke to wash my hair. My big fantasy moment. I was going to be Meryl Streep and he was going to be Robert

Redford and he was going to wash my hair. Except I couldn't move without pain. And I certainly wasn't feeling romantic. I had just had my breasts removed. And I had these weird temporary breasts (tissue expanders) in their place. And my chest was numb. And my underarms hurt from having tubes in them for a week.

Because I hadn't properly showered I still had purple Sharpie hieroglyphics all over my chest. And I had no nipples. And I had big scars and stitches in place of each breast. And a small, angry scar with stitches under each armpit where the drain had just been removed. Let me tell you . . . this was clearly not how I envisioned beckoning my loving husband to come make my little movie scene a reality.

Now, don't get me wrong. Had I called him from the other room, he would have done it in a second. He would have been there for me, washed my hair, and not made me feel the bizarre, odiferous (!) freak I felt at that moment. And I would have loved him for it. But I did not want him to see me like that.

In that moment I had a dilemma. What kind of woman was I going to be?

What kind of person was I going to be with this disease from that moment going forward?

I was going to push myself. Do it myself.

I wasn't going to be taken care of if I could help it. I knew I was going to have trouble asking for help, have trouble accepting help. I knew these things were going to be necessary. But I also knew they were going to cause me problems. That's the kind of person I am.

I knew asking for and accepting help were actually going to make me feel weaker than I was already feeling. And it was only the beginning. I knew these actions were going to make me feel weaker than I knew I was going to get. I wanted to do everything myself for as long as I could.

That was what was going to make me feel alive: doing it myself.

I am not sure I did the best job washing my hair. I probably missed a spot or two. But I did it. And I didn't ask for help.

Granted, it was something small.

But in that particular moment, on that particular day, that particular act gave me a feeling of pride as big as anything else I could have possibly accomplished.

January 29, 2013

No Manual

I always think these updates must be boring to read. I know they're necessary, and important. I know this is how most of you get the nitty-gritty details on my treatment. Somehow, though, I always wonder if they are actually educational or if they are too technical. So, that's why I try to limit them to about once a week or when there are changes. My goal is to show you how these decisions get made (in my case only).

Some cancers have very specific and formulaic treatment schedules. Metastatic disease often does not. It's unclear which drug(s) will work and for how long. It's never known how a patient will tolerate the drug initially and cumulatively as time goes on. The patient has a lot of leeway in many of these cases. There is no blueprint. A good team has communication about options and constantly revises their strategy.

I had this week "off" from chemo. The last few days I've felt very good. I have been spending lots of time with our new dog, Lucy, who has brought joy into our home in so many ways. We just adore her.

I was at Sloan Kettering last week and today I met with my local oncologist. Fortunately everyone is in agreement after a review of all of the options. One of the things that's always a concern is quality of life. My doctors are very keen on making sure I am comfortable and able to do things I enjoy. The balancing act of aggressive treatment to extend life without sacrificing too much quality of life is an integral part of treating metastatic cancer. There is no cure. But the goal is holding off the inevitable as long as possible.

We've achieved a good decrease in the last four months with the Xeloda but now that is slowing down and I seem to have "bottomed out" on its efficacy, what now? We want to keep everything where it is. If we can get more of a decrease, that's the best. If not, we need it to hold steady. We all agree it's time to try again to increase the chemotherapy dose and see if I can both tolerate it and get a stronger marker response.

It's time to walk into the fire again. We all brainstorm, we talk about what my goals are, we talk about what makes scientific sense. We'll see how I do. Debilitating nausea, stomach pain, hand/foot syndrome, and migraines have been my issues with this drug in the last month.

Also, I will change my start day. Thursday night was my usual. Lately, however, I've felt rotten on the weekends. I will now start chemo on Saturday night or Sunday morning and see if we can shift my "rotten days" to weekdays instead. I want more quality days with my family on weekends if I can get it.

This is all educated guesswork, a constant dance of drugs and schedules and side effects and efficacy.
There is no manual.
There is no "must."
There is only me, floating away, trying to grasp the fingertips of treatment and hope.

January 31, 2013

Floating Away

I sit on the beach, feel the sand's angry texture rub my chemo feet in a way I wish it wouldn't.

I watch my family in the ocean, turquoise and calm and vast.

My husband flips over, face in the water, takes some strokes out to sea. His movement is graceful, effortless, just as it was when I met him twenty-two years ago.

He was a sprinter on the college team then, and while he laughs and says it doesn't feel effortless anymore, nor perhaps fast, it does not matter. In my mind's eye he is that young man, swimming fast, joking with his team, coming over to the stands to talk to me while chewing on the strap of his racing goggles. I fall in love with him again every time I see him swim.

My three children float, bobbing in the ocean water.
I can feel the distance between us; it feels like a lifetime.
It is my family in the ocean floating away from me.

I see the quartet, I watch as an outsider.
I do this a lot lately. I watch them from afar and think how it will be without me. A new family unit. Behind the big black sunglasses my tears stream down.

Suddenly Tristan is running from the water to me, across the sand. He stands, dripping, face beaming. "I just wanted to tell you I love you, Mama." I take his picture. I capture the sweetness. I grab him, hug him, feeling the cold ocean water on him, melding it to my hot skin. I murmur to him what a sweet boy he is, that he must never lose that. I send him back to the ocean, away, so I can cry harder.

By the time they return to shore I'll have myself composed. But my oldest immediately senses something amiss. She mouths to me, "Are you okay?" And pantomimes tears rolling down her cheeks.

Yes, I nod.

I walk to the water's edge to prove it.

April 18, 2013

The Sound of Startled Agony

The response to my last post, "Floating Away," was truly overwhelming. Thank you for your responses, comments, and emails last week.

I wrote three pieces while I was in Florida. I was planning to take time off from writing, to focus on the trip, the family time together, the joy. And I did. For most of it. The truth of the matter is that even joy right now is tinged with sadness. The writing I did was on my phone and was explosive and emotional.

That's just the way it is. What I'm doing is grieving.

It's been six months since the diagnosis of metastatic cancer. I've already run through one chemo regimen, wrung its effectiveness dry, and now have had to move on to something else.

The loss of control is hard. It eats at me. I always wanted to believe that if I played by the rules, took the most aggressive route I could with my cancer the first time (more than six years ago), that I'd at least be NED* for a decade or two.

---

*   I never have used the term "cancer-free" since it isn't necessarily accurate. Some like to say they are cancer-free after they finish treatment for breast cancer. This is not always the case. In some cases there are residual cells, as there obviously were in me. These cells stay dormant in some people for decades—maybe the rest of your life—and hardly dormant for any time at all in other people. 30% of those who've had breast cancer that isn't diagnosed originally as stage IV will ultimately have a metastasis where the breast cancer cells leave the breast and travel to other sites in the body. Only metastatic breast cancer can kill you. Rather than "cancer-free" I have always preferred the aforementioned term NED. This stands for "no evidence of disease." The difference is that this term acknowledges there may still be cancer cells in the body, but they are not currently detectable on any tests. Maybe there aren't any. Or maybe there just aren't enough to show up on the tests.

I was told my chance of recurrence was in the single digits. But cancer doesn't listen to statistics—good or bad. The features of each person's cancer are different. How aggressive it is, its resistance to certain treatments, its mutations.

I am not a risk-taker by most definitions of risk. I always felt that playing it safe would somehow benefit me.

I have come to believe that what I did actually *did* matter. I have come to believe it's not that *it didn't work*. My surgeries, chemo, prophylactic oophorectomy . . . maybe, just maybe, those things bought me a few years. It's possible I'd be dead already if I hadn't done them.

I digress. But I want to reiterate that just because I am writing heavy pieces here, this isn't the way you will find me if you see me in my daily life. There is joy, happiness, *living.* Please know that. I've always explored the darker emotions, the harder subjects.

Perhaps I feel the written land of the upbeat is for others. My niche is here, in the agony of this disease. There is so much emphasis on "being positive" and all of that; I feel the compulsion to show the flip side, too. I do not want to show the nitty-gritty details of what the cancer is doing to me, what my side effects are, what appointments I go to; while important, they are a laundry list. Instead I choose to do what I have been doing all along here: writing my way through the forest of my emotions.

Sometimes as I'm drifting off to sleep I make a sound. A sudden hmmmmm or a series of loud breaths.

If my child did this as I watched her sleep I'd furrow my brow, stroke her hair,
pull up the blanket and tuck it under her chin.

But who will do that for me today?
I push them away, it is not time yet.

I do not yet need to be cared for like that.
And yet, I know it will come.
I must fight these demons.
I brave the fear.

I agonize with the decisions.
I push harder than I should.
They are watching.

Always watching for a chink in the armor, a sign of weakness.
No one else can truly understand what each of us with this disease must balance.

Even those of us who have chosen to publicly share our lives with cancer still manage to keep much of it to ourselves.
I do.
I must balance privacy and pain and catharsis.

Many people say they still can't believe my stage 4 diagnosis.
That denial is a luxury afforded to those who are not compelled to live it.

You must believe it.
We must believe it.
I must believe it.
I have no choice.

It's my life now.
It's my death someday.

That noise I make as I fall asleep?
It is the sound of startled agony.

April 21, 2013

Some Days

Some days I say to myself, "Enough with cancer."
Some days I say, "That's enough. No more."

No more thinking about it.
No more doing.
No more helping.
No more advocating.
No more educating.
No more communicating.

But then I say, "There's still so much to do."
There's still so much to say.
There's still so much to hope for.
There are still so many who suffer.

And so I am pulled back in,
Writing, talking, sharing.

Some days I want to talk about anything but cancer.
But I remember this is the new me,

This is my new life.
This is who I am.

And as long as there are others who come after me,

I will do what I can . . .
to hear,
to help,
to hope.

January 6, 2011

Dealing with the Topic of Death

Despite the fact that it is the one thing that unites us all and is the one common thread in all our lives, most people just don't want to explore the subject of death. It makes people uncomfortable, makes them squirm, and almost universally makes people change the subject.

When you have had a death in the family, people don't know what to say. In fact, it is likely many people won't bring it up. Often, they worry that they will be reminding you of the tragedy, as if you have forgotten it. Anyone who has experienced a death of a loved one knows this isn't true. The deceased person is never far from your mind, from your heart. And more often than not, you want to talk about that person. My mother taught me this. She taught me that people will never be upset if you remember and talk about the person they loved; it means their legacy lives on. Everyone wants to be remembered. You honor this desire when you talk about a deceased person.

Often when I was in the midst of chemotherapy I wanted to have conversations about the "what ifs."

What if they didn't get it all.
What if the chemo doesn't work.
What if the cancer comes back.
What if I get another (worse) kind of cancer from the chemo.
What if I die.

No one really wanted to talk about the last possibility even though it wasn't outlandish.

I viewed talking about my death as responsible. I wanted to make sure Clarke understood that if I died, I wanted him to find another wife. I wanted him to be happy and loved. I wanted our children to have a mother to love them. Unsurprisingly, my greatest worries centered on my children.

I sat with a friend at coffee one day and voiced some of these concerns. At first she was resistant to talk about my death with me. She didn't want to entertain that notion. But I pressed the issue. And finally she looked me in the eye and said, "If you die, I promise I will watch over your children. I promise I will make sure they have the right person love them and raise them. I promise you that I will make sure that happens." I think she figured it was the fastest way to shut me up. I think she figured she would agree to anything I was asking just so we could get off the subject. But at some point I think she realized that it was really important to me. I wasn't going to let it go. And I wasn't going to be able to get past it until I felt they would be safe and watched over. So she told me what I needed to hear. And I know she meant what she said.

Like a balloon slowly deflating, I felt my body go lax. Finally, I could let it go. She had promised me she would do for me what I wanted. I could trust her, and I could move my worry to something else. She did more for me by making this promise than she will ever know.

Here is one of the things I've learned from my mother: When someone you love is talking about death, don't change the subject. Don't trivialize their worries. Don't say, "Let's not talk about that now." If they want to talk about it, it means it's important to them, it's weighing on them.

Focus on the fact that while we don't need to sit around thinking about death all the time, there unfortunately might be times in our lives when we might not be able to think of anything else. If you haven't experienced that, I applaud you. But sooner or later, you or someone you love will.

December 14, 2011

Dragging My Feet to the Finish Line

The finish line is the goal.
Runners strap on shoes, push their bodies, train for months.
Do it well. Do it faster. Faster than the others.

Laps around the track, tires squealing, pit stops along the way.
Checkerboard flags, shake the champagne.

Biking stages, climb the hills, pass the others, wear the gold
jersey.
You got there first.
You won.

But I do not want the finish line.
I do not want to get there first.
I am dragging my feet.
Digging in my heels.
Fingertips grasping,
Losing touch,
Don't make me go.

I'm fighting, crawling, resisting, doing everything I can.
Make the time slow down,
Make the days longer,
Make the end out of my sight.
I don't want to be the first to the finish line.
I want to be last.
This time, losing would be winning.

February 11, 2013

Waiting for the Seasons

When I was diagnosed with Stage 4 breast cancer last October
I could not envision the future. I wasn't sure if I even had one.
Or if I did, for how long.

It has been four months now. Some people don't even get four months after a Stage 4 diagnosis. But I am here. And my cancer is responding.

Last October I wouldn't let myself think about spring. Or summer. Or a three-year renewal on a magazine. I'd wonder if I would outlive the expiration date on the can of food I'd put in my grocery cart. I renewed my son's USTA membership for ten years and hoped fervently it would be my job to renew it in a decade, not Clarke's. I wondered if I'd see out the rest of my car lease. I just didn't know what to expect.

In some ways I still don't. My future is unknown. But that is good, I'm coming to think.

When I go to an appointment with my oncologist and he isn't changing anything, telling me it's time to try a different treatment, or handing me a piece of paper with a list of scans, I am happy.

We are hoping to find the "sweet spot" where I get therapeutic efficacy but still have manageable side effects. That's the goal.

My oncologist talked about another goal for me today. We both know for now these two-week intervals are needed. But one goal he would love to achieve is even more stability with my body's response so that I can have longer stretches of time between appointments. Having bloodwork, checkups, and my monthly bone drug (Xgeva) all at once would be grand.

When he told me my results I said, "That's a two-week reprieve." He said he wants me to be able to think in longer increments. I'd love that too. I'm thinking about seasons now.

Spring.
Summer.
Autumn.
Next winter.
Beyond.

Let's go for it. Let's make plans. Let's see what happens.
Together.

February 15, 2013

If You Let Me

Once or twice a week I awaken in the middle of the night with
a poem in my head. I reach for my phone and I type franti-
cally. I go back in the morning, or after a few days, and read
what I've written. I know the words are important, streaming
from my head like water breaking through a dam. This poem
came from one of these middle-of-the-night sessions.

If you let me
I'll cry you a river
Scream at the moon
Hold your hand
Kiss your mouth
Feel your heartbeat
Dream of more
Fear the end
Wish it were different

Pound my fists
Swear a blue streak.

If you let me
I'll give you strength
Find a reason
Deliver some hope
Take a needle
Feel the pain.

If you let me
I'll be grateful
Feign bravery
Take a stand
Do my best.

In the end
I'll whimper softly
Try again
Give a last kiss
Take a last breath
Slip away.

March 4, 2013

The Still of the Evening

In the still of the evening I hear the frogs waking up to spring.
I hear the creak of the floor as my daughter walks around her
room,

Sets things just so,
Murmurs to our dog.

In the still of the evening I hear a car,
A train,
A neighbor calling his own dog home for the night.

In the still of the evening my mind wanders again.
Back.
Always back.

I finished my thirteenth round of chemo forty-eight hours ago.
I wonder what is going on inside my body. I wish I could see.
I wish I knew.

Is it working?
Is this round the one that will show evidence of chemo failure?
Will I move on to a new treatment?
One step closer to the end?

Every time I bang against something,
Every time I feel a twinge,
Every time that fractured bone aches,
I pause.

The pauses add up to moments.
The moments add up to minutes.

I reel them back in like fishing line, I show them who's boss.

Just listen, I say.
Listen to the frogs. The creaks. The murmuring. The train.

Just listen.
Just hear the quiet,
Hear the house going to sleep for the night.
Feel the love.
Be grateful you can.

April 9, 2013

Quicksand

When you're in it
You can't see your way out.

Some days the only thing that gets you through is thinking
All days can't be this bad.
They will get better.

But what happens when you reach the time when they won't
get better?
It does happen,
Eventually.

Each time you sink in the quicksand
You're never sure if it's the last time you'll be able to get back
up.

Pretend each time you will rise.
Just get through this spell.
Imagine it's just another in a string of bad days
That will be followed by a good day,

Or two.
Or three.

That's how you get through the days, weeks, months, years...
If you are lucky.

There is no option to me.
There is no alternative.

Up. Forward. Onward.
Even when it hurts.
On the outside.
On the inside.

March 11, 2013

Clarification About End of Chemo + New Plan

I want to just send out a quick clarification about my chemo because I can tell from messages I'm getting that I didn't explain well what has happened with my discontinuation of Xeloda. This particular chemo is now failing, yes. *But that doesn't mean it didn't work.* This is part of this disease of metastatic breast cancer. In some cases the treatment option never works; that is, your cancer doesn't respond at all. You get no benefit from day one. You abandon it quickly.

Mine, however, falls into the other camp: it did work for a period of time. It did what it was supposed to, just not for as long as we'd hoped. That is, it did reduce the amount of cancer in my body for a while, it did hold progression at bay.

It's no longer doing that; my counts are very slowly rising, but that doesn't mean it "didn't work." It just means it didn't work for as long as I would have liked.

Most people with advanced disease will be leapfrogging around all sorts of agents (chemo, anti-hormonals, etc.) to try to see what works. The cancer mutates and becomes resistant to most treatments that will get used. That's when it's time to move on to a different one. I know people that have been on at least ten different agents. That leapfrogging is just the nature of the path many others and I are on. A small percentage find one that works and it continues to work for a long, long time. Research is needed to find out why these particular cancers are more easily tamed. We do not know now why that is the case but researchers are learning more and more about the subtypes.

So while the stability was not as long as we'd liked, in this particular case it doesn't mean it didn't work. It did. For six months. But now we're moving on.

April 12, 2013

Expiration Date

It is easy to be happy when you are healthy.
It is harder to know that this may not be true much longer.

People love to casually say,
"Enjoy every moment" or

"We all die some day anyway" or
"Life is fleeting."

I know this already.

And I know it in a different way.

I don't need to be told to
fight the good fight to beat it
or the key is to just stay strong
or that it's mind over matter
or that I should pray for a miracle
or that I will be cured.
That's nonsense.
Scientifically impossible in my case.

And so, when you say,
"No, that can't be true.
There must be something that will cure you,
If you want it/pray for it/think it will be so,
You can be healed,"
What you do is force me to assert my knowledge,
Insist upon my diagnosis,
Explain the desperate nature of my disease,
Spend my time defending my sentence.

I know it's what you wish.
I know you insist because you want it to be the case.
I know you're grasping at straws,
Wanting to reassure yourself that bad things won't happen to
you,
That bad things don't happen to good people,
That something awful won't happen to me.

Trust me, I wish for it too.
But these things do happen.
It has happened to me.

The truth is that wishes don't count for anything when you're
placing them against cell biology.

I know many healthy people who say the passage of time is
bittersweet.
It isn't a competition but I can tell you that this passage of time
is different.
If you could feel it for just a moment you would know.

There is a difference between
Distant,
Hypothetical,
Potential,
Maybe . . .
and reality.

I have learned that being nervous about test results,
Worrying,
Wondering,
are not the same as the reality.
Reality is having your oncologist walk in the room
and when you say to him, "How are you?"
and he says, "Not good,"
you naïvely think it must be a problem with him,
or his family and
instead he ducks his head,
takes a breath,
looks at you, and says,

"Your test results were not good.
Your tumor markers are up."
He knows I know what this means.
He waits for a moment and says,
"I think you have a metastasis."

A few minutes later he says,
"You need to go get a chest x-ray right now.
Go across the street,
I will come over to the hospital and look at it immediately.
Wait for me there.
Then you need to schedule a PET scan as soon as possible.
Have you had any other unusual pain?
A cough perhaps?"

The room spins, the world stops.
My life didn't end in that moment, but life as I knew it ended
for sure.

No turning back.
Reeling, processing, shock.

All you can do is let your jaw drop,
the tears fall,
your body shake,
crumple.

Slowly,
deliberately,
as I looked at him
in a way that I never had in the six years he had been my doctor,
the only words that came to my lips in response
were to repeat over

and
over
and
over
and
over
again:
"Fuck. Fuck. Fuck. Fuck."

Because that's the only word that could capture how angry
and scared
and angry
and surprised
and angry
and shocked
and angry
I was.

I never have liked the term "to expire" rather than "to die."
I started thinking about these words though.

We all have an expiration date.

I've never thought of it like that before.

We all have one.

It is as if I've grabbed a carton of milk without looking.
I took the one in front I guess,
The one with the rapidly approaching date they put conve-
niently at the shelf's edge for people to grab when they're not
paying attention.
Except I did pay attention.

I did.
I was always paying attention.
No one was more vigilant than I.

I want to put this carton back,
I want to say it's not mine.
I want to scream it.
This must be for someone else.
The date is too soon but I can't trade it in for a new one.
No givebacks.

The problem is
I don't know exactly what the date says.

April 28, 2013

Out of the Water

This afternoon I will attend my youngest child's Field Day. It
will be a steamy 93 degrees here and I will join parents as we
stand around and chat while we clap for our children and hug
their sweaty bodies and remind them to drink lots of water.

It is always in these group events that so many of us feel like
outsiders. It is often when surrounded by many people we are
most aware of being alone. For me, this has never been more
true than during the past eight months since my diagnosis
with stage IV breast cancer.

I return again and again to the desire to escape, the need to
flee, the pull toward being somewhere else. The refrain in the

new song I am co-writing with Doug Allen is about this need we all have, regardless of the cause, to take moments during the day where we just "check out" for a bit. It says:

I take a trip inside my head,
I don't know where I go.
Somewhere else,
Anywhere else,
Far from things I know.

There are days when I want to be the ostrich, when I just am so overwhelmed with things that I can't be on social media, returning emails, or even talking. I just am still. I notice that I rarely read anymore; even television can't capture my attention. I sit in silence a lot, and when I have the opportunity I write or work on the songs.

I take those trips inside my head.

The pull of educating and informing is too strong to allow me to stay hidden away, though. Social gravity pulls me back. Sharing and documenting fuel me. I take my anger, my sadness, and my grief and I send them out into the world in constructive words and deeds. I can feel powerless and without control in many ways about what is happening to me but I always feel that I can control my reaction to these things. This is my lesson to the people in my life.

There is a scene in the film *Children of a Lesser God* where William Hurt's character jumps into a pool to try to experience utter silence the way that his deaf girlfriend does. He wants to know what that *feels* like. He quickly realizes, however, that this won't work. He knows when he rises to the surface he will once again hear sound. He can't live what she lives. He can't share her loss in that way.

Antoine de Saint-Exupery wrote, "It is such a secret place, the land of tears." Most mornings I stand in the shower for a while longer than I need to. I listen to the water, I think about the day, I am grateful to have another. I know I will have more days. For those few minutes I take a trip inside my head. I gather my strength, I focus on the work to be done.

I turn off the water, I step out of the enclosure, and I rejoin the world of the living. That's what I am doing every day: *living* with metastatic cancer.

May 31, 2013

No Room for That in This: Six Minutes

I find myself in silence a lot,
Tuning out the noise.
No room for anything but thoughts.

I try to forget for a few minutes,
I stare at a spot on the wall.
I lose myself.
No clue how long it has been.

The clock says it's been six minutes,
I am glad that they've gone by.
But then I realize I have wasted them:
Six minutes of my life.

I want them back,
Feel I should use them for something better,
Something constructive.

I am mad at myself:
That was a waste of time.
I want days of suffering to pass,
But I also know that this is the only time I have.

I take a trip inside my head
I don't know where I go.
Somewhere else,
Anywhere else,
Far away from here.

If you'd let me, I would run away,
I would go find a way
To keep you safe from this,
Safely far from this.

Some days I long to tell you how I truly feel,
But there's no room for that in this,
No room for that in this.

It is not a choice.
That I know.
And when I finally do go
It won't be for lack of want, or heart, or strength.

When I die it will be because that is what cancer is,
This is what cancer does.

And when it comes to being fair,
There is no room for that in this,
No room for that in this.

May 15, 2013

[Note: Lisa's friend Doug Allen wrote music to this poem, and they worked together to create the song "Six Minutes." You can hear the song on YouTube at http://bit.ly/six-minutes-song]

I Just Want

I just want to see my son play baseball,
Watch him wave at me when he's on base.

I just want to take my daughter shopping for makeup,
Applying powder to her porcelain skin.

I just want to read with my youngest one,
Snuggled up in bed together turning pages of a book.

I just want to grow old with my husband,
Continue to share our lives as we have for twenty-two years already now.

I just want to sit in the garden when we are old.
I just want to talk about the good old days.

I don't want to read about mTOR inhibitors or side effects or months of disease-free progression.
I want to read beach fluff and skim through cheesy magazines.

I want to get a pedicure and have a nap in the chair.
I want choosing the color of my nail polish to be the toughest decision I have to make for a day.

I don't want to read reports from the ASCO conference or tweets about new research findings.

I just want it to go away.
But it can't.
It won't.

I will never know another day of my life without metastatic cancer or chemo or treatment or dread.

But I will search for joy.
I will.

I will do what I can every day to find that joy,
And if I can't find it I will make it.
This is my pledge,
This is my promise.
For them.

Some days it is hard to do.
Some days fear and sadness are too much.
Some days I do not know how I will do this with grace,
But I will try.

I must make the most of this time:
Helping others, educating, writing.

I know no other way to do this.
But it's the hardest thing to do.

I cry, I give in to the emotions, but only for a few minutes.
No good can come from that.
I gather strength.
I re-commit.
I go on living.

The bad days will come someday.

But that day is not today.
That time is not now.
And so I am a parent, a wife, a friend, a sister, a daughter, a
writer, and everything else I have been until now.
That is who I am.
That is who I will continue to be.

For as long as I possibly can.

June 4, 2013

Worry Beads: Hang on, Baby

I have my list of things I worry about.
First on my mind in the morning,
Last in my head at night.

And if I pop awake in the middle of the night?
Yes, the list is there too.

Across the aisle from me on the train to New York City last time sat a woman.
At one point on the journey she flipped huge black bug-eye sunglasses from the top of her head down over her eyes, her look now an insect dressed in designer clothes.

She reached in her purse,
grabbed a strand of worry beads and started kneading them.

With a rapid-fire reflexiveness she started moving one bead at a time.
Each only moved about half an inch down the string.
From the worry side to the safe side.

I could hear the rhythmic mantra of the beads again and again and again,
Quieter but still audible over the clickity clack pattern of the train itself.

I wondered what her worries were.
I wondered if she would add mine to hers.
Or trade with me, even.

Sometimes we need to do something with that energy.
For her it was tiny movements, thumb and forefinger
Pinching and sliding ivory beads on a round string.

We have our rituals when things get bleak. Some pray.
I do not.

There is a coping that comes with grief, a way to release the tension that grips us when things are bad.
Some days it does feel like it eats from the inside out.

When you must come to terms with what you fear
and what you dread
and all you want to do is lay down on the floor like a petulant
two-year-old
and kick and scream about the unfairness of it all . . .
As if the universe gives a damn that life hasn't been fair to you.

Clearly it doesn't.

So I do not appeal to the universe to change what is.
I turn to my balms. I turn to research.
I turn to science.
I turn to determination and hope which are the last things I
can cling to,
fingertip by fingertip,
like the cat on that iconic poster that says "Hang on, baby."

Inner strength is sheer will.
My claws are firmly entrenched.
There is no other way to be.

There is no justice.
It's up to me to come to terms with the weighted side.
That is where I live right now.

And so every day, when I wake up in the pre-dawn hours and
contemplate my worry list and
come to terms with the day that is about to dawn,
I gather strength,
summoning it from its slumber.

"Here we go," I say.
"Let's do this."

Another day is here.
I will see another.
Hang on, baby.

Of One Kind or Another

I never learned how to juggle. I never could master the coordination of having control of one thing while letting go of two.

And yet, in my life, I am asked to do this daily. Three children, a husband, a house, the constant ebbs and flows of life and family and the demands those things take. Add stage IV breast cancer to this mix and it's a daunting task at best.

"Too painful to think about" is something others can afford to say or think about those like me.

But I cannot. My body does not let me.

Perhaps having hair, looking healthy, betrays me.
Perhaps people forget what my body is enduring.

Perhaps they forget on a daily basis the struggle it is for me to do what I need to do. On some days the hardest task I have is the mental component of trying to deal with this all.

They do not know that while I drink my coffee in the morning and type an email I am prone to worry. I wonder if pain in my side or my back or my neck is cause for concern. I am mentally comparing the location of the pain to the bright flashes on the latest PET scan. I try to remember my body's details on that scan. I create a split screen in my mind. I contemplate if the spots align, if they don't. I have memorized the words in the radiology report. When I want to torture myself I recite them.

There is no "moving past cancer" anymore or counting down to the end of chemotherapy. There will be no day of claiming victory and yet my victory is defined by each day. Winning is not possible, its re-definition now just seeing how long I can keep running, outsmarting the cancer that's here to stay.

I waved a triumphant flag six years ago. I was done with surgery, treatment. My chances of a recurrence or worse, a metastasis: small, small, small. Single digit. The odds were in my favor. "Look where those odds got me!" I scream inside.

I serve as a terrible, disturbing reminder to those just starting treatment: you can't be sure. You can't get cocky. You can't ever be positive that you are done. Perhaps you live your daily life that way, but it can happen. Even years later, it can happen.

That wily son of a bitch can lay in wait, cells silent, dormant for a while. And then, when you least expect it, spring forth to attack, to ravage, to ruin all you know is true. This is why I bristle when people with my particular kind of cancer say they are "cured."

I hesitate when people ask me how I am.
I know they want to believe I am okay.

Even for today.

They want to believe there will be a happy end to the story. But there cannot be.

This is not my middle age. I will not be that lucky. While others complain of gray hair or wrinkles or saggy bellies I long for them. I want to earn those badges.

I want to flaunt my age.
But let me flaunt a number that begins with a 5 . . . or 6 . . . or more . . .

I now know this is why my doctor had that look on his face when he told me the news last October that my cancer had metastasized. This is why, when he gave me the news, he let me cry and swear again and again and again when every word in the English language but "Fuck" left my vocabulary.

This is why a particular doctor I know looks at me with sadness in his eyes when I see him, when he hugs me, when he tells me "you look good."

That doctor looks at me like that because he has the curse of knowledge: *he knows how this will go.*

He knows. He knows this story, he sees it daily. He knows what's coming. He doesn't want me to see the ending but it will come. All we are doing is pushing the "pause" button as many times as we can. When I hug him I feel it. The regret. The pain. He knows what waits for me. It makes me sad to see him in the hall sometimes, as if that feeling can be transferred between us in a look, a hug, a touch. But that compassion, that pain . . . well, those are honest moments.

Perhaps I ramble today. Perhaps my weary body and mind make no sense. Perhaps I should hit "delete" and send this down the drain. But this is all part of my story. If I am feeling it, I know somewhere someone else can relate to it too.

Every day is a struggle of one kind or another. I am doing the best that I can.

And oh, how I wish I could forget. How I wish I could forget.

July 14, 2013

A Flash of Red: Happy Birthday to Me

A flash of red amidst the green summer grass:

a lone leaf, blazing in autumn clothing, a vivid premature announcement of a change of season.

Perfectly waxy, thick and juicy, it could not have been there long.

It is, I realize, the color of my mother's lipstick. The color she has worn every day of my life. Perfectly fitting for the moment...

I turn forty-four today.
I do not know how I feel about this fact.

The day I turned forty-three was a lifetime ago, surely not just one year. I did not know I had metastatic breast cancer then. I was ignorant and blissful.

I had no idea what my life would be when I reached this birthday.

I have no way to know what it will be when I reach the next. I do believe I will see it though.

I am in limbo at the moment, waiting in the next few weeks to see if my current chemo has stopped working. I do not know if I will need to move on to something else to try to buy myself some time.

That is, you see, my only wish: more time. That is what I wish for today.

Time with my husband. Time with my children. Time with my parents and brother.

Time with my friends.

Chances for memories.

Opportunities for more.

I will keep trying to give a face and a voice to this disease.

There is poetry in the human experience.

I will keep trying to find it, document it, and also help others.

One way I have tried to help is by setting up a research fund.

I am glad to see forty-four. But there is inherent sadness in birthdays now.

Cake,
balloons,
the wish that comes true if you just close your eyes and blow out the candles . . .
if only it were so.

And so there is an anachronistic flash of red,
a moment of color.

I am that leaf,
released from the tree before its time,
floating downward,
coming to rest where it has no earthly business being,
nestled in the green summer grass.

July 29, 2013

The Story I Cannot Edit

This is the last week of summer before school begins.

This summer was a big one for us. Youngest Tristan went off to sleepaway camp for one week and loved it so much that in the end, he stayed for a month. Paige and Colin returned to camp as seasoned veterans and had a wonderful time in their home away from home. All learned new skills and made new friends. Paige and Colin's constant banter of camp stories at the dinner table are now supplemented by Tristan's own stories.

I'm so pleased they could be in a place where they could just be kids, not worried about me, free to be carefree and happy. It is my gift to let them go, to not keep them here for my own needs. While I want to spend as much time with them as I can, I know that this is what they all needed to do this year.

I sit back and smile now, loving that they all have a common reference point of their weeks at camp. Despite the eight-year age gap they all find laughs and joy in their summer adventures. They look older to me, of course. And while others are sad about the passage of time and their children growing older and being independent, I say again that I cheer it.

You see, my job now is to prepare them for life without me. My goal is to show them how to accept the help of others but not be reliant on it. I choose to show them every day that there is determination and nobility in facing what life throws you. You may not be able to change the final outcome, but you can change what you do to be ready for it. The strongest way of teaching this right now is by living my life deliberately, making choices and showing them the best I can be. This doesn't mean denial. Nor does it mean I don't lose my temper or raise my voice or fall apart sometimes. To be emotionally numb or invariable in my response to what is happening is not healthy. I try to show them that expressing what they feel is a better option. Emotions of anger and sadness and grief and fear are fine to have. It's beneficial to talk about them, but dwelling on them won't make things better. Acknowledging their reality, their truth, their basis is what's needed.

As I always say when I get bad medical test results: a short pity party is good. Then you have to pick yourself up and move on.

It has been almost eleven months since my diagnosis of stage IV breast cancer, and there isn't a day that goes by that is free from concern. I notice myself being more and more affected by the daily chemotherapy, feeling more fragile, more vulnerable. I have already had one bad respiratory illness this summer, and I worry about the school year and all of the potential colds and infections that will be transmitted. I don't want to think about the ways cancer affects my daily life, but I must. The decisions I make about activities, treatments, and chemo all directly affect my life... both in length and quality.

I push myself to do the most I can. I try to do all of the little things that add up to a full day: school supply shopping, back-to-school haircuts, camp laundry, new shoes, sports registrations, and walking the dog. I also request meetings with school administrators, coaches, and anyone new in my children's lives for this fall that need to know how my kids' home life differs from the one they had a year ago.

I'm a planner. I take comfort in routine, the familiar, the predictable. Unfortunately, those are now removed from my life forever. Yes, I know life always tosses everyone curveballs. That's what life is. But I experience it in a whole new way. I have no way of saying life will ever return to "normal" or even a "new normal." There will not be a "better." I am not "sick" in that I cannot recover.

I still feel the drive to help, to counsel, to educate. But am finding it more difficult. I hate saying *no* but know I will need to start saying this more. In-person interaction is very difficult for me. While no one would know it to look at me, social interaction is extremely draining these days. I try to minimize contact knowing that when I am in public I am under scrutiny. People want to know how I am. They want to be reassured. They look at me for clues as to how things are. There is no reassurance I can offer. This is a disease of progression to the end, a story that will not have a happy ending.

I want the story that I am living to be a good one, to the highest degree it can be. I want the story for my family and friends to be one full of love, memories, and devotion. These people are the center of my world.

I want the story to be different from what it has been, different from what it will be.

As a writer I am used to editing. Revising. Changing what I don't like.

But I can't edit this story.

I can't start it all again.

And so I write through it.

The only way out is through.

But this one . . . well, this one is quite simply going to have a sad ending, as many stories do

August 20, 2013

The Beggars Have All Ridden

Remember me pretty,
Remember me whole.

Remember me the way I am today
While friends still honestly say, "You'd never know."

Let me tell you:
It's not what it looks like,
It's not what it seems.

Those times are long over,
Now I am on my own.
The beggars have all ridden.
My wishes: horses gone.

I float above it all,
Watching as I do.
Surrounded by people,
Feeling so alone.

Head down,
At the stoplight tears come,
A young man pulls up next to me
Glances once . . . twice . . .
With an engine rev, he's gone.

I hide it pretty well, you see.
They say, "You look so good,"
"You are so strong,"

But in the space that's in between

I fall apart
I kick and scream
I claw and grab on for dear life.

Because really,
Truly,
What is happening here:

Choice is gone,
Chance is Queen,
Luck will run right out.

Everyone placed their bets?
Let's see how far we can go.*

August 29, 2013

Like a Summer Child

I'm not about to let myself go.
I'm not about to stop wearing makeup or dressing nicely or
styling my hair each day.
I'm not about to relax my standards or let my children get
away with things they shouldn't.
I'm not about to stop being a friend, a daughter, a mother.

I'm not about to stop having dreams.
I'm not about to stop learning, growing.
I'm not about to stop sharing.

I can't just give up.
I can't stop moving.
I can't change who I am.

---

* Note: "If wishes were horses, beggars would ride" is an English-language proverb and
nursery rhyme, originating in the sixteenth century, which suggests if wishing could
make things happen, then even the most destitute people would have everything they
wanted.

I know some of these things will change.
I know someday soon I won't have choices about what I do
each day.
I know there will be a day I won't have hair to style again.

I push myself too hard each day.
I feel I am in a race against a clock.
I must pack as much into each day as I can.

I am in constant motion,
Like a summer child waving her arms to keep the mosquitoes
away . . .
I dance and thrash and run away,
Looking for a place to escape injury where there is none.

I can't control so many things about having metastatic cancer.
This feeling is one of the hardest things about this disease.
But those things I still can?
I'm holding tightly onto those,
And I'm not about to let go now.

September 19, 2013

It's Complicated

Alone.

Willing myself to recharge, gather strength, get ready, be
stronger.

Chemo starts again. One more week.

My relationship status with chemo on Facebook would read: It's complicated. Chemo keeps me alive. Buys me time. Gives me days, weeks, months.

But makes me sick. Causes my hands and feet to numb, get tender, peel, redden, swell, ache, burn, throb. Tires me, sickens me, weakens me.

How can I hate that which gives me hope?

I cannot decide if stage IV means I must downsize my dreams or shoot for the moon. Is there nothing left to lose or simply nothing left?

March 13, 2013

A Cacophonous Roar

There comes a moment in many conversations,
I can see it:
They reach their limit.

Ten minutes in, or maybe only five,
They start to drift off,
Squirm,
Just want to be done with it.

Sometimes they even say,
"Let's talk about something else" or

"Let's change the subject"
Every so often they go as far as to say, "This is depressing."

Being done with it is something I would love to do.
I'd love to tell the inner me to forget about it.
But that's not possible.

It's not mind over matter when that matter is making you sick,
as are the treatments you need to fight it.
Metastatic cancer is background music, but it is a cacophonous
roar.

I put it in its place,
But it has a place.
And the fact that it even has a place,
Well, that is just the way it is.
I try to keep its place as small as possible.
For as long as I can.
But I don't have the luxury of changing the subject or forget-
ting about it for a while.

Like a greedy child metastatic cancer demands attention.
I tell it to wait,
Give me a bit of a break.

First I demand it.
Then, worried, I ask again contritely.
Then I downright beg.
Please, just give me some more time.

But I don't believe there is anyone who hears me.
I don't believe there is a god listening,
And I don't believe cancer gives a damn about it all.

And so the plea evaporates as quickly as it came,
The tree in the forest with no one to hear.
I can only do my research, try to make the best decisions.

But in the end,
These cells will do what they will,
As they have,
Without respectful regard to all of my attempts to banish them.
That's not how it works:
You can't wish them away,
Hope them away,
Love and light them away.

Cellular biology is King.
But paired to that fateful ruler
I shall be an argumentative, rebellious Queen.
Wring the most out of each day.
Find those bits of joy and beauty,
Make sure that what I'm doing isn't waiting around to die.
For truly, that would be a waste.

And in those conversations now I am grateful there can be other subjects to move on to,
Share the lives of my friends and support them,
Even if I am simultaneously pretending I can't hear the roar.

The greedy child still tugs at my hem,
Will not be denied.

I needn't let that noise drown us out,
And it won't silence me just yet.

October 7, 2013

Find a Bit of Beauty

I must do the best I can given my daily symptoms. There are question marks and only time will give us answers. I try to have as much normalcy as I can, which often just feels like sleepwalking through the days and a bit of play-acting. But it's important.

I can't do anything more to change what's happening inside. I have a plan and I just need the days to go by to get started. My quality of life is suffering at the moment but I hope that this will change. It is a rollercoaster, one I have been strapped inside unwillingly. Some days are good, some days are not. These happen to be some of the icky ones, but as always, I press onward.

Every morning I say to myself:

Find a bit of beauty in the world today. Share it. If you can't find it, create it. Some days this may be tough to do. Persevere.

October 18, 2013

One Step Ahead

I know I shouldn't always attach explanations on posts like this but today I feel the need to. Whenever I post a dark piece I get many messages of concern (and criticism) from people. Sometimes they say, "Lighten up." Most often readers are worried. I want to say that these pieces capture only a fraction of the spectrum of feelings I have.

My days are not spent wallowing in sadness. When I need to rise to the occasion I do. It's often easier for me to write about the world of the dark places though . . . in some ways I think those are the ones that need light the most. These words are often the ones which go unwritten and unexplored.

I always find joy in the small moments each and every day. Today I tweeted, "I find beauty in the flowers in my room, the sight of the leaves through the window, the sound of the wind, the loyalty of my dog."

There is shimmer in each and every day. Some days we just have to look hard for it, dig deep. And some days there is just a darkness overhead. I find that giving a voice to those depths, shedding light on them, is important. There are many who live in this land. Today's post comes from the feeling of doom that accompanies test results, that awful waiting period.

I wait for the burlap bag over my head,
Wait for the rope round my neck.
I wait for the chair to be kicked out,

The floor to drop open,
Snapping the rope's length and my body with it.

This is what it feels like each time I drive to the office,
Head into the building,
Take a seat.

Usually I hate traffic
But when it slows my journey I find myself grateful these days.
Stretch out that time.
Make it longer until I hear words I don't want to hear.

They are tricks, of course,
Silly childish games I play.

I turn on the heated seat and press my back against the core
Burning relief into my spine.
I am at war with myself.

I ready myself to smile, to say good morning,
To greet the office staff with a brave and carefree smile.
"How are you?" one will ask,
Letting the words roll off her tongue the same way
The lady with the Irish accent ringing up my groceries asks me
Without waiting for an answer.

I'm not fine.
I'm anything but.
There is no time for that, though.
It's time for results and plans and tests and exams.

It's time to steel myself again,
Stand up straight,

Pretend there is no fear,
No ache,
No catastrophe.

For minutes at a time this is how I get through the day.
I walk at a clip, slightly faster than that executioner with the
bag and rope who chases me,
One step behind or maybe two,
Telling him
No.
Not today.
Just stay the hell away from me.
Just for a little while longer.

October 26, 2013

Morning Chat: Will You Have It Forever

"Why do you have to have surgery tomorrow?" seven-year-old Tristan asks from the back seat after we drop off his eleven- and fifteen-year-old siblings this morning.

"Because I need to have something put in my body called a port. It's a little container made of something cool called titanium that lets the doctors put some of my medicines into my body in an easier way."

"Can you see it?"

"Yes, you will be able to see that there is a lump under my skin, about the size of a quarter. But you will only see the lump.

You won't see the actual thing because that will be inside my body. You know how I have the scar on the front of my neck? It will be like that, here, off to the side, same size scar but with a bump under it."

"Is it like the bubble I had on my neck when I was a baby?"

"Well, that was a skin tag, so that was a lot smaller. And they were taking that away. This is something they are putting in to help make it easier to get some of my medicines. And you know when you go with me and I have blood taken from my hand? Well now sometimes they will be able to just take it from there instead. So it helps with a few jobs."

"Will you have it forever or do they take it out when your cancer goes away?"

(Driving the car, trying to keep tears in check, knowing this is a vitally important conversation. I've explained this to him before but I know it's hard for him to understand.)

"Well, honey, remember I had cancer when you were a baby? Well, this time the cancer is different. A lot of the time you can have cancer and the medicines and surgeries make it go away and it stays away for a long, long time. Maybe even forever. Sometimes any cancer cells that might be left go to sleep and just stay that way. Sometimes you have bad luck and they wake up. Mine woke up after six years. And now the cancer cells are in places that I won't be able to get rid of them all for good. I am always going to have cancer. This time my cancer is the kind that is always going to be here."

"You'll always need medicine. And the thing they are putting in?"

"Yes, honey, I will always need medicine for my cancer. And I will probably need to have the port in forever too."

Long silence.

"I am glad you are asking me questions about it. I want you to always ask me anything. I will try to explain everything to you. I know it's complicated. It's complicated even for grownups to understand."

Long silence.

"Mom, did you know people whose eyes can't see use the ridges on the sides of coins to tell which one they are holding? So if you have a big coin with ridges that person would know it is a quarter?"

"That makes sense. How did you learn that?"

"At school. And so if it's smooth you know it's a nickel or penny. It's important that they know what coin it is."

"I think you're right. That is very clever."
(I stay quiet waiting to see where he will take the conversation next.)

"Remember when my ear tube fell out and was trapped in my ear and the doctor pulled it out and I got to see it? It was smaller than I thought it would be."

"Yes, I thought the same thing."

"I really wanted to see it. I wanted to see what it looked like."

"Me too."

"Can you show me a picture of it?"

"Of what?"

"The thing for tomorrow."

"The port?"

"Yes. Or don't you know what it will look like?"

"I know what it will look like. Sure, I will show you on the computer after school."

"Okay."

"It's time for school but I am glad we talked about this. I want you to keep asking questions when you don't understand something. I love you, Tristan. I hope you know how much. I know this is hard for all of us. I wish it were different. But we are going to keep helping each other. And talking about all of this is good. We can do that whenever you want."

November 21, 2013

A Fragile Time of Year

We are entering a fragile time of year. The holidays are difficult for many people. Some miss loved ones who have died. Some mourn their own lives, no longer what they were. Grief takes many forms. The pressure to create memorable and uplifting occasions can sometimes be oppressive.

Be kind to those who are struggling during this time; physical and mental illnesses can be especially difficult to manage. Understand that happiness and sadness can coexist. Reach out to others if you can.

Find a bit of beauty in the world. Share it. If you can't find it, create it. Some days this may be hard to do. Persevere.

November 26, 2013

We Are Not There Yet

"This one has to work," she says. "It just *has* to."

These are the words my phlebotomist says to me every time I see her. She says it strongly, willing it to be so.

I wish it were that easy. If wanting it could make it so . . . all of the people who send their support in prayers, thoughts, hopes, vibes, whatever it is *they* hope will help . . . all of those would work. And yet, here we are. Through no fault of theirs, or mine.

It is important to see the larger picture here, aside from my own life. It is important for everyone reading this blog post to know that despite all of the hype and exclamation points and strong language about a cure or the promise of successful long-term targeted agents for metastatic breast cancer so that it can be more like a "chronic disease," *we are not there yet.* The number who can live like that are the minority. Most live in this life-and-death game of Whack-a-Mole that I do now: metastases ("mets") pop up, and you try to bash them back down but as you do they pop up somewhere else.

The state of metastatic breast cancer care is that you can't just test your breast cancer, look on a chart to find the drug that will work and always shut it down. Metastatic breast cancer has eluded this formula so far. We don't have drugs yet to even target every mutation. And we don't know which inhibitors work. Most work best in combination with other treatments and we have to have clinical trials to test all of those options. All of those things take something those of us living with MBC don't necessarily have: the luxury of time.

Cancer is complicated. It has multiple pathways to get fuel. Block one? It finds another. And even when you have a drug that shows results in mice or in a few other people, you don't know if it will work for you. There are too many variables, too many drivers of cancer in complicated feedback loops.

You can see where this is going. I have come out on the wrong end of the equation yet again. The trial drug combination did not work.

But we have other more serious concerns now. We now have confirmation that the pleural effusion is larger than in the last scan. In plain terms, there is cancer in the pleura (the membranes around the lungs) that is producing fluid that builds up in that normally thin sac beyond what can be drained by the normal body process.

Additionally, my liver is now affected as well, unfortunately. There are multiple lesions that are metastases as well. This is obviously something I was hoping to avoid for a while longer.

The nature of metastatic breast cancer is that you don't know how fast things will move or where the cancer cells will settle and thrive. They like the environment of soft tissues (liver, brain, etc.) so these developments are not surprising nor what I want to be hearing.

We need to get aggressive in a new way now. Anti-hormonal agents and inhibitors have not been working for me even though on paper they "should." Treatments that logically should work might not. And that's why I get angry when some very visible people in breast cancer care want to keep talking about how "close" we are to personalized treatments and even cures. The research has yet to support that idea. In fact, the latest research has repeatedly shown how complex the interactions are. We now know there are more than thirty subtypes of breast cancer. And even those subtypes don't always respond alike to treatments.

Cancer is wily. And I hope I'm wrong about how far away we are from true leaps and bounds in MBC care. But I know I won't see it in my lifetime. For how many decades now have we been hearing about those "breakthroughs" and "miracle drugs"? Yes, they've come in some cancers. But not MBC (metastatic breast cancer). Reporters and health care professionals in the public eye need to monitor how they spin info about the current state of metastatic breast cancer treatments.

Let's not send the message out about how "close" we are to a cure when there isn't research to back it up. Let's not send a falsely reassuring message out there that metastatic breast cancer doesn't need much attention because soon we'll be able to make it like a chronic disease anyway. Until we have actually *done* that, we must push full steam ahead and not encourage complacency in research.

December 18, 2013

In Each Equation I Calculate, the Result Is Always Time

When even television seems too much,
And hours go by staring out the window.

I listen to the sounds of my children playing,
I hear life go on without me.

It was a day like this that I wrote the lyrics to the song "Six Minutes."
A day I wished for the time to go. Just *go by faster*.
But as on that day,
Today I am aware that these are the days I'm fighting for.
If I didn't want them I wouldn't be doing all of this.

I know that this is a tough day. Tomorrow will be one, too.
But I also know that someday, hopefully long from now, it will count as a good day, a great day. And that realization scares me too.

I spoke with a patient care representative at Sloan about some of the mistakes that were made on Friday. I told her my story and we talked about some ways she could follow up. I told her I wasn't angry, I know mistakes happen, but I thought there were ways to try to make sure these things didn't happen again. At the end she gave me her contact information. I said, "I love my doctors and the care I get. But there are always ways to improve. I appreciate the chance to give those suggestions to someone who can do something about them."

Then I started laughing. "You know, I hope to be calling you with suggestions for many years to come. That will mean I'm still here, trying to help patients get better care and trying to help doctors and nurses provide it." She started laughing too. "You know, I really like that perspective. I'm not sure I've ever heard it put that way. I like thinking about more suggestions as meaning more time." We thanked each other and hung up.

And I thought about it.
Everything is an equation now.
Everything is a calculation.
Everything has a cost.
I try to balance risks.
I study statistics and results.
But in each equation I calculate, the result is always time.
Nothing is more valuable than time that I am able to enjoy the world and those around me.

December 23, 2013

Marking Time in Cancer

After I was diagnosed the first time with cancer in 2006 I began to mark time in a new way.

The parent of a newborn starts with days, then weeks, then months and fractions thereof. "How old is the baby?" a parent is asked. "He's five days old" or "Eleven and a half weeks old" or "Sixteen months," the reply will come. But when that child is a teenager no one will mark his age in days and half weeks and months. The importance of those fractions will fade. Once he's got years under his belt their significance is muted.

Time now gets marked in rounds of chemo, time elapsed since diagnosis, months without disease progression. There's always a mental countdown, a cognitive calculation going on.

I find myself obsessed with time in a new way, but also rapidly losing track of it. Granted, some may be chemobrain. I wonder now that I am on chemo for the rest of my life what it will mean to my brain. It's a necessary evil, but concerning. The chemo that kills cancer cells is also killing brain cells. New evidence shows the reality of this condition, no longer a punchline or mere excuse for forgetfulness.

I always encourage people with cancer (and any illness) to keep a calendar of their treatment. There is so much to keep track of that having an easy reference point is good. When did you change doses of medications? When did you see certain side effect symptoms? Jotting them down in a calendar or noting them in a smartphone calendar can be helpful. Sometimes on paper, patterns will emerge.

Grief is such a wily companion. Like smoke it creeps into places when offered only the tiniest access point. Grieving the life we thought we'd have is important. It's easy to say, "Lives don't always go the way we plan," but that undermines the emotional complexities of dealing with serious illness. Just because things don't go as planned for many of us (most of us?!) doesn't mean there isn't a serious adjustment to make.

"Roll with the punches" and "live in the moment" are deceptively simple phrases of advice that are not only absurdly emotion-free but also easier said than done. More than once in the past few weeks I've challenged people whose best words of support have been to live in the moment. While I understand the ideology, and agree with the premise that we must enjoy the time we have, I defy anyone without a stage IV diagnosis to tell me that it's the quality of your years, not the quantity of them. These are things that healthy people say. Yes, quality matters. None of us want to suffer. I don't. But years count, too. "Living in the moment" can imply that the grief process should be squelched or has an expiration date. Anyone who has experienced grief knows there is no expiration date.

Of course none of us knows our future. Some people try to tell me they don't know their future either; they could get hit by a bus tomorrow. I love the response that Jen Smith suggested, "Would you like to trade odds?"

Acceptance of reality must come. Dwelling on the dark side of diagnosis won't lead anywhere productive if dwelling is the only thing one does. I think that is the real meaning behind the idea of focusing on today. The acceptance of reality does come. Of course, that's complicated when the reality of one's prognosis is unknown. I have quickly built up tolerance for discussing the most serious and unpleasant ramifications of my condition. I occasionally sleep through the night. But I don't know how long it will take to wave goodbye to my children in the morning, or tuck them all in at night, or talk about the future without feeling pain with the joy.

I mark the time. I'm back to being someone who counts the months and weeks and days. Counting them, appreciating them, grieving them. All at once.

December 14, 2012

Adjusting the Best I Can

The last weeks have not gone as planned.

I had the liver biopsy and PleurX drain put in my left lung on 12/31/2013. I was going to only stay one night for observation and to try to address the pain that I was having. Further tests revealed more information. The pain that we thought was coming from my lung and spine wasn't just coming from my lung and spine. In fact I have some tumors in my bones in the left hemisacrum and right femur too. The spine tumors are now in more vertebrae than we'd thought.

I've actually been in the hospital for six days now trying to get the pain under control and formulating a treatment plan with my team. I will need to be here for a while longer. I am starting ten sessions of radiation later tonight after being mapped this morning. We had hoped to do it in five sessions but for reasons I can't go into now they have decided this is a better route and will be more effective for the future.

This treatment will stop the current progression of pain, but the way this radiation works for me is that it won't provide true pain resolution for probably about two weeks and then improve further over the next few months. The pain reduction will be cumulative and take a while (long after the radiation is actually over) to see final resolution in my case. I'll have to deal with this for a while yet.

The side effects because of where they are targeting the beams in my spine will be irritated esophagus, trouble swallowing, nausea, vomiting, and heartburn. The other radiation site in my hips will potentially cause decreased blood counts, pain, irritation, gastrointestinal pain and dysfunction and the like.

My pain is still not under control and I'm on a Fentanyl pump system that allows me to dispense medication as needed in accordance with the pain levels. I will convert over to oral medication and patches when it's time for me to go home once we can figure out my needs. The pain and palliative care team here is unbelievably caring and devoted. So are the physicians and nurses. I have created an expanded family here already and can't say enough nice things about the quality of care and total commitment to the patient.

I think for now that's enough news.

Please, please respect my declaration that I do not want uninvited visitors, any gifts, or any flowers sent during this time. I know the intent might be good, but I appreciate so much those who have opted to instead donate to my Sloan Kettering metastatic research fund instead of purchasing anything for me. I haven't been able to send thank-you emails for those recent donations but trust me, they are appreciated. Good thoughts are also always just fine and have the right price tag!

This is a time when I am dealing with severe pain, a medical diagnosis that is unfolding and serious, and needing rest as much as possible. I do read emails but I am not responding to most at this time.

I was not able to start the clinical trial because of these newest announcements. We will see if I am eligible for it again in the future but for now we have to get the disease and pain under control. I did go on chemo for a few days but it now needs to be stopped during radiation. I will resume chemo after radiation is over and about a week of recovery time has elapsed.

Things change hour by hour, day by day. I'm adjusting the best I can. I hope this will at least let you know where we are, a long way from where I thought I'd be in the first days of this new year. Welcome to the world of metastatic breast cancer.

January 6, 2014

Adhesive

I add another ball of surgical tape to the back of the photograph of my family hanging at the foot of my bed.

Don't fall.
Stay there.
Just stay.
Together.

I wake up fettered, chained, restrained in body and mind.

The room is cold and yet it stifles:

Choking, pulling, grabbing me back, reeling me in.

I start to shake, fear manifest in movement,
Waiting for Reality,
The next interloper . . .
Another who will not be pushed away,
Ignored,
Wished or willed or
Bargained for.

I search for powers to rise above, get out, fly away.

Those dreams cannot escape that reality.
That shaking cannot stop.

When repeatedly pushing the button of narcotics is an act of acceptance,
A realization of what is,
In part an impotent attempt to eject myself from the room, the bed, my body.

The tears which accompany my pathetic try stay safely tucked away,
Hiding with hope and mental acuity and certainty.

Like middle school children the fear starts to divide, partners off, chooses a companion for the evening.
Two by two, hands on hips, turning tightly into a circle
Guarding spots of possession,
Declaring ownership,
This is mine.

The fetters must remain and yet I will not budge.
I have my spot.
Small perhaps,
But it is still mine.

I have my life.
I watch it shrink.

I have my words.
But now I see them dissolve around the edges
Like watercolors they bleed as they search for pristine lands to conquer
As they stretch that lifeline.

The words of disease become words my brain gravitates to.
The ebb and flow of cancer,
Of life.
And so too,
Inevitably,
Of death.

Each night when I return to my room after radiation now it happens:
My voice instantly is quiet, reverent.

I am respectful of what I ask that beam to do,
I ponder the magnitude of something I cannot see.

And so I affix that photograph, one more piece of tape just in case.
Holding on to all that matters,
Doing as much as I can for as long as I can.
Day by day,
Storing up bits of beauty wherever I can find them.

January 8, 2014

Target Practice

No matter where you are
There is always beauty in the delicate unfurling of the morning as
It and its inhabitants come to life for the day.
A chair scrapes on the floor upstairs,
An electric bed adjusts,
An IV pump sounds,
A shade gets lifted to see the twinkling city.
A soft voice enters the room,
Two pills in a plastic cup down the hatch without disturbing a keystroke.
Vital signs are taken, the velcro cuff rips.

Vials of blood from my port,
The soft tapping of the tubes as the tech manipulates them
deftly in one hand to keep refilling constant.
An IV pole whines like a morning toddler standing in her crib,
anxious for first attention of the day.
Toilets flush,
Breakfast orders placed.
Young doctors start to trickle in to find out how each patient's
night went.

And then some of the real business of the day starts.
Decisions made each day about life and death.
Who has surgery today,
Or a chemo change,
A transplant,
Biopsy.
Some will go home, some will not be ready.
News will be given.
Each person has a life unfolding here today. But remember it is
a *life*.
Not a diagnosis, not a body part.

But just as the tide goes in and out,
Gives and takes,
So does metastatic breast cancer.
It progresses, taking more,
You hopefully have an arrow left in the quiver to try.

You tame it back and do the dance again. And again.
Leapfrog through treatments trying to stay one step ahead.
There is always adjustment.
It is a shifting target. You'd best be on your toes.

I am at the beginning of what treatments are available for me. Don't you count me out yet. Far from it.
Just because this disease can't be cured doesn't mean there isn't a lot of life left in me; there is still so much for me to do.
I am living with cancer.

I want to count the days until I can be home and *me* again. But we do not know exactly how many are left. Getting closer I hope. When I get back home it will be a different me, but that is not the point. This is part of metastatic breast cancer and now I've had my first introduction.

It's been fifteen months since I received my diagnosis. This is the first time I'm needing any type of radiation. I will have to pull out some more aggressive weapons in chemotherapy options. But as I've done each time, my oncologist and I will research and discuss.

The discovery in the past two weeks of more metastases was a curveball. But it's standard practice for metastatic breast cancer. Totally typical.

I have quickly come to care for the people who work on the floor. There is so much care and assistance and tenderness every day. I could not be more grateful for the daily affection mixed in seamlessly with medical care.

Each room has a story.

My room has smiles and laughs and love. It has tears and anger and bewilderment. It has every part of life.

As I attack the cancer cells in my body I must always search for ways to bridge to the outside world. My family and friends have made that easy. They are my heart and soul. The supporters I have online help so much too. Your words of compassion and care keep me going and remind me why what I'm doing is so important. Using the time I have now while I am able to be functional is precisely the point . . . continue to give those too weak or unable to share the true experience of daily life with this disease a voice. To teach, to enlighten, to share, to support, to fundraise for research . . . and to always honor those who have died.

As always I could not do any of this without my oncologist, Dr. Chau Dang.

There's always so much more to say. But I've got some time to do that.

Thanks again for the support I receive from so many of you. You know how much I treasure it: it's my beauty.

Find a bit of beauty in the world today. Share it. If you can't find it, create it. Some days this may be hard to do. Persevere.

January 9, 2014

Places of Refuge: Walking the Pole

The car has always been a place of refuge for me.
The shower, too.
Water to rejuvenate

Clearing away the old,
Ready for a new day ahead.

The moment of awakening is significant.
I have learned quickly what the next few hours will be.
I try to give a nurse a complete report but I encounter one problem immediately.
I really cannot type accurately.

My body shakes, my hips cry out in bony futile gasps. I gather up my pump cords, release myself from the wall's grip.

I walk, counter-clockwise around the nurse's station with a vengeance, trying to push the pain and discomfort away.

I am angry at this morning and that which has me here.
The tears arrive.
The radiation pain seems to be on the way in.
How long will it last? Does that mean it's working? I and everyone else ask.
"I don't know" is the way to do it. I say it aloud to the dark, embarrassed after the first word that I realize I am alone in the room.
I hear my voice, speaking to someone not present.
I can't help but cry as I push the pole.

The movement makes it better. It reminds me of being carefree on a summer day, wind in my hair from the sunroof, feeling the sun on my face.

I think of my friends readying their homes for the day before work and school.

I can feel the radiation, where it burns, or at least the spots where tumors are trying to escape their home, where they try to find new lands to conquer in a cat and mouse inside my body.

It doesn't matter what stinking metaphor you use for it; in this case, all roads lead to Hell.

I contemplate eyeliner while the nurse stands, patiently waiting to see how I've done overnight.

...But there is no one there.

I focus very hard on the tasks at hand: morning medicine most especially.

I start to tell my nurse that I weighed myself already today. Or yesterday. Or two days ago. But I can't remember now. And so I remain mum.

In each moment my mind leaves. I don't know where it goes. But in those gaps which feel like seconds, minutes have gone by.

The tea is divine, hot silky relief from the cold my body cannot push out.

I realize whatever it is I thought I could accomplish at the keyboard won't happen once again.

I can't concentrate. I find gibberish on the page. It takes hours to do a few moment's work.

Extra time lost.

Time lost.

My precious time.

I stay committed to sitting up, bedside, fighting the urge to recline.

I listen to music trying to keep myself alert.

I think about my children, wondering what each is doing...

I realize today I am too foggy from medication.

I won't be able to do much for a while. I am too busy talking to people that are not there.

I will rest, let the pain calm, let my head settle.

January 10, 2014

Where Have the Days Gone?

The pain that was so debilitating is finally under control with pain patches. It takes quite a high dose to keep it managed right now but we will try decreasing this amount as the weeks go on. I will meet with the palliative care team in a few weeks to talk through a strategy for the reduction. The team is always available by phone for any fine tuning or questions that I have until that time.

Again I'd like to remind readers that palliative care is not synonymous with end-of-life care. Palliative care is for pain management and side effect management at any point of treatment for cancer or other diseases. If you have pain or other problems that are bothering you or a loved one, I encourage you to talk to the specialists in palliative care. They will be able to help.

Patients and their families often wait too long to consult with these specialists because they think talking to them implies something about death. It does not. In fact, if you wait too long (until the very end of life) the palliative team will probably be less likely to fully help you or your loved one because they won't know how the patient responds to different medications, what their side effects are, what doses they respond to, etc. Palliative care doctors can help better if they know the patient and their particular side effect profile. I implore you to use them sooner rather than later. Time and again, studies have shown that healing occurs better when patients are not in pain.

February 7, 2014

Good Ones and Bad Ones

It's been about three months now since this particular acute metastatic breast cancer episode started. First I was stuck at home in pain with tumors in my spine and hips before and during the holidays. Then I was in the hospital for three weeks at the start of 2014 getting pain under control and having two weeks of radiation. Now I've been home for another six weeks since leaving the hospital.

After such a long period of time many people will start to assume you "must be back to normal by now." Each day they anxiously wait for news that someone "feels better." It doesn't work like that all the time, just the way with metastatic cancer you don't "beat it." A good day or two may come, but they are often followed by a bad one, or two, or three. Add chemo to the mix and you start to realize the good days are relative and elusive in incurable cancer. Support is always so appreciated as the days, weeks, months go by. It's friendship for the duration.

There are many situations where isolation may be a real danger including examples of infertility, chronic illness, and grief. Those who must deal with these problems start to feel isolated. Additionally, they may start to actively separate from others when they feel that life is just moving on without them. As time goes on, they may hesitate to talk about their problems because they fear that friends will have grown weary of hearing about it or still can't relate to it. More and more, they keep these things to themselves. This leads both to further isolation and also the faulty notion from their friends that the person is "over it."

The truth is that it's very hard when difficult situations of all kinds linger. I think we all do better when tough times are brief. Being in one of these situations has shown me the depth to which this is the case.

Today I had to miss Tristan's spring music show at school. It broke my heart to tell him I couldn't attend. They were able to videotape it and I know we will watch it together and have a special time doing that. If it were just one thing it would be different. But as any parent can imagine, saying, "I'm so sorry but I can't..." again and again for months is difficult. The truth is that if I knew it were temporary it would be easier. But I know that there will be more and more things I can't do with the kids. And that's what weighs on me: this thing is part of a whole.

I tried driving last weekend but unfortunately, for now, the verdict is that I am still unable to do more than go to the bus stop at the end of the street if needed. So I continue to be housebound.

I'm working with my doctors to adjust my medications and try to manage the vertigo, sedation, and pain. I am using less pain medicine (hooray) but unfortunately I still feel so rotten I sometimes can't get out of bed and most often can't go anywhere except to chemo. It is a cruel balance. This weekend I was stuck in bed for three days. It saddens me to lose so much time.

I still long to write here more. I miss the creative part of my brain working the way it used to. I miss poetry and photography and so many things. I will bring them back though! My friend Alex brought me lunch and a beautiful potted orchid. I even ordered daffodils with my groceries this week to remind myself of the garden outside and what's waiting under this snow.

Winter break at school came and went. I know it's a very busy time for everyone as spring approaches. It's hard to see life outside passing me by while I wait for spring so I can at least get fresh air here at home. It has continued to be cold and wintery over the past few weeks. If you're able to be outside today doing anything: errands, standing at the bus stop, or waiting on the train platform on your way to work: think for a moment what it would feel like not to do <u>any</u> of that for three months. It's a very long time. Mundane things can be sweet when viewed in a different light.

I am so grateful for the offers of help and meals that continue to come. Let me assure you they are so needed and appreciated.

March 4, 2014

In These Last Remaining Hours: Camp

In these last remaining hours
Before my children disappear

One,
Two,
Three . . .

In these last remaining hours before they go and spread their
wings again,
Leave this nest,
I miss them already.

I put the dinner pots and pans away.
Wipe the crumbs from the table,
Load the dishwasher,
Play fetch with the dog.

I sit in the garden,
Listen to the wind in the trees,
The birds settling down before nightfall,
As we settle, too.

I tuck them in one last time,
Hear their doors click shut.

One,
Two,
Three.

Tomorrow night there will be no mess to clean,
No yelling upstairs that the TV has been left on again,
No trunks piled high with carefully labeled belongings in the
dining room.

I will cry, I know.
Not because I am sad that they are going—no, that gives me
great joy.
Children being children.
Forgetting stress at home and doing new and varied things.
I cheer their independence.

I will cry because I know they will always need me somehow
and I just wish I could be there for them to outgrow
by choice,
by time,
by age.

I hear the mother bird in the tree calling out.
I don't know to whom.
I will be like that tomorrow,
calling out,
with no child to hear.

June 22, 2013

Like Dollhouse Rooms Left Abandoned

Like dollhouse rooms left abandoned,
The rooms stay tidy:
Beds made tight,
Pillows square,
Hampers empty.

It's been one week since the children left for camp.
Littlest Tristan was due back yesterday but a few days ago he
said he was having so much fun he wanted to stay another
week.

I realized this week that after being sick for the previous two
that I needed this time to catch up, to rest, to regroup.

I miss them but am so glad they are having fun doing what
they love.

I pack up care packages,
write letters,
wake in the middle of the night and mentally picture our children sleeping in cabin beds.

Our dog, Lucy, follows me, sleeps in my room now, not Paige's.
She doesn't want to be alone and stays within feet of me every
moment.

I tell her it's okay:
The kids will come back.
The rooms will get messy again.
There will be crumbs dropped at the dinner table and car rides
galore.

Paige and Colin and Tristan will come back tired and dirty and happy.

They will come back.

They will.

That is the key.

I think of absence like a hole:

How different it is when it's temporary and filled with happiness,

Rather than when that hole is a pit of grief. Of ache. Of loss.

The way it will someday be for them.

July 1, 2013

Summer Camp

We will get to see the kids this weekend and I can't wait to hug them and hear all of their stories before they go back. They love camp, always have. They look forward to it year-round and now that they all go it's great they can share these stories and experiences (they are fifteen, twelve, and eight. Last year the youngest begged to go for a week to try it out. We said yes, knowing his siblings would be there and he would have a blast. Five days in he called in tears, begging to stay. That repeated every week until after a month we said it was time to come home!).

Some may wonder why, at this time, I let them go instead of keeping them home with me. I do it because it's not about me. It's about them. It's something they love. It's an important routine, tradition (this is the sixth year for the oldest). In my eyes, it's important that they have a change of scenery, freedom to be *kids*, get away from the ways my cancer and its chronic treatment limit what I can do, and therefore what *they* can do. It's a gift I can give them and I also feel it reassures them that I am doing better than I was a few months ago. This is important.

I love having them away from electronics, away from wondering if asking me to take them somewhere or do something with them will be "too much" or "bothering me" which I know the older ones are always concerned with. I want them to be with friends old and new, having fun with young and energetic counselors, trying new things. There are so many (most/all) physical activities I cannot do with them that they can do there. So many new games to play, achievements, laughs, experiences. I never hesitated when they were ready to sign up last October for this summer. I knew that no matter what, they needed and deserved it.

That doesn't mean it's easy for us to be apart. We are very close. Especially the older kids worry about me I am sure. But I stay in touch by email, will see them on visiting days, and I send them weekly care packages.

But the truth is that separation is good. It's a selfless act for me to teach them how to be without me. One of the most important things, in my mind. Coddling them and making them stay home is not what I feel is best for them right now. It is part of our job as parents to teach our children how to be independent, how to solve problems on their own, how to go off in the world without us for whatever reason. *I will always want more time with them. It will never be enough for me.* But this is my old age. *I must teach them as many lessons as I can, while I can, for as long as I can.* And that is true for everyone, but of course I have not only the urgency to do it NOW but also I have no idea how long I have and will likely be debilitated in some form until that time comes.

Yes, it's true no one knows how long they have to live. But those diagnosed with a terminal disease know what is most likely to kill them. And that their time is not just going to be shortened, but consumed daily with the treatment and effects of that disease. It's not having a normal, healthy life that is relatively good and healthy until a sudden accident happens. It's just not the same as the general worries of growing older or aches and pains. It's never-ending. I don't get to count down how many chemotherapy (or other treatment) sessions until I'm done this time. Being done will mean there is nothing left for me to try. Anyone who has had chemo or radiation or some other type of therapy knows how important it is to have an endpoint, a countdown. Knowing that will never happen (and in fact what you're really hoping for is a lot of them, because that means you still have options) is one of the mental struggles each week, since it isn't just spending one day a week getting chemo, it's how it makes you feel each day after that.

July 9, 2014

Give Sorrow Words:
A Guest Post by Dr. Rita Bonchek on Helping Children Understand Death

The following is a piece my mother wrote this week at my request. Dr. Rita Bonchek spent her career as a psychologist specializing in grief and loss. There is no one I know who is as insightful into the grief process as my mother. So much of the information I share was gleaned through years of listening to my mother talk about these subjects.

My mother gave me the gift of discussing difficult subjects with relative ease. I never could have known how they would come to play in my own life, most recently with the death of my mother-in-law in 2009 and my stage IV cancer diagnosis this October. She has written posts about the difference between guilt and regret and other topics.

We all will have experience with grief and loss. It's a universal part of life and yet most people find themselves poorly equipped to handle the emotional and practical aspects of the death of a loved one.

After the killings in Newtown, Connecticut, I asked my mom if she would be willing to write anything for me to post on my blog. I know so much has been published in the past eight days about children and their grief, but I have opted to give my readers the opportunity to read what she says. Sometimes different posts on the subject will resonate differently. I hope you will find helpful information here.

In Dr. Rita Bonchek's words:

Helping children, especially the very young, to understand the death of a loved one is never an easy task. Not only do children's perceptions of death include confusing images which lie between fantasy and fact (as when cartoon characters are killed and then recover instantly), but children's vocabularies are inadequate to express their feelings and fears.

The following are suggestions to help you help your child:

1. If the death was unexpected, convey the facts in a straightforward way. Be sure to answer the who, what, why, when, and how questions. You will probably have to repeat the facts many times as your child struggles to understand what happened. If you want to check on what your child knows about the death, ask him or her to tell you what happened. Encourage your child to come to you or another designated adult when questions arise.

2. Talk about things your child has already noticed but might not understand ("You know I've been crying a lot. It isn't anything you've done. Sometimes I think about Grandpa and I cry").

3. Give your child permission to cry by modeling that behavior or by saying, "When I cry it makes me feel better."

4. Use the word "died" and be sure the child understands the finality of death. One child said to his mother, "I know Daddy is dead but when is he coming home?" Children are unable to deal with euphemisms such as "eternal rest" or "We lost your uncle today."

5. Be sure to convey the clear message that the death was not the child's fault and there was nothing that he or she could have done. A child's words, "I wish you would go away and never come back" or the thought, "If I didn't have a brother I could have all of the toys or all of Mom's attention" do not cause a death.

6. If your child asks a question that you don't know the answer to, say "I don't know" or ask what he or she thinks.

How a parent handles his or her own grief has a definite impact on how a child grieves. If a parent does not mention the death, avoids all discussion of the event, and/or removes pictures of the deceased, the child will easily follow these cues. You can't protect a child from hurt or sadness by pretending nothing happened and hoping the child won't notice. Children sense when something is wrong.

A child can also be overwhelmed by a parent's excessive grief, which, unless it is given proper explanation, may serve as a source of insecurity or leave a child emotionally abandoned. If you cannot help your child to grieve, be sure someone is available to provide understanding, support, and information.

Parents cannot assume a child feels nothing about the death just because the "adult" forms of grieving are absent. Some children may quickly resume play activities which gives the appearance of not caring, but they will "quietly" cry into their pillows at night. Play may be an attempt to discharge anxiety, to distract one's self, or to find relief from the sadness of thinking about the deceased.

Research has shown that children and adults grieve in different ways from each other. However both adults and children should abide by Shakespeare's advice:

> Give sorrow words; the grief that does not speak
> Whispers the o're fraught heart and bids it break.

Unresolved grief can interfere with a person's ability to function. Those adults and children who can work through their grief and express their emotions openly, hopefully with each other, as much as possible, will be stronger and better able to lead full and satisfying lives.

December 22, 2012

Curtain Falling

They were already seated when we arrived, a sea of white sitting cramped.
Mostly couples, though some were in girl groups.
They didn't rise when we needed to pass by.

Clearly that effort would be too much.
I know how that feels.

Almost all wore glasses, most eventually pulled out bags of snacks or sucking candies.
No one texted or emailed or checked the time on a phone.
They all had small watches on their wrists for that.

In front of me a man had a bandage on the top of his head, white gauze perched amidst his silver hair, a good head of it.

I decided a funny-looking mole, irregular in shape, had lain there recently; his wife pressed him to go see the dermatologist to have it checked.

The two looked out for each other, you see, having been together so long.

The air was still and thick and choked me as the minutes wore on.

I could see the veins protruding on the back of their hands, the wrinkles, the hunched shoulders.

We were the youngest there.

And while I felt more like them in many ways, closer to the end than to the beginning, I realize I am an outsider in every group.

There are few like me.
My hair won't get that white, you see,
My hands won't be rewarded with that saggy skin.

I won't be privileged enough to see him go bald.
It will always be "in sickness" now.

The lights finally went down and I tried to forget.
But my body and mind do not ever let me.

How jealous I was of those elderly people crowded into a
movie theater on an August Sunday afternoon.

August 4, 2014

Little Words

Grow up faster,
Need me less,
Reach the sky,
Stand up tall.

Make time go,
Speed it up,
Get it done,
Don't look back.

Hear my voice,
Feel my embrace,
Know I tried,
Look straight ahead.

Keep forging,
Thinking,
Feeling.

There is no choice,
This world is all there is,

Make it last.

Ours will be far shorter a time than it should be:

Years compressed into months, days, hours, minutes.

It will never be long enough,

It simply could never be enough time with you.

August 22, 2014

Hard to Hear

The last week was stressful. Unfortunately, my bloodwork shows that the chemotherapy regimen of Carboplatin and Gemzar is losing its effectiveness. It's time to start looking at options for what to do next.

We watch my tumor markers very closely and check them each chemo cycle (every three weeks). Once there is evidence of an increase in the marker number, my oncologist and I start to construct "if/then" decision trees. I know from earlier this year how fast metastatic breast cancer can spiral out of control. I don't want to have that happen again if I can avoid it.

There is no guarantee that any given treatment will work. Many chemotherapies won't work at all. One that works in 50% of cases is considered a great option. If they do work, they won't keep working. The cancer will mutate, become resistant. We seem to be there again.

There are options to consider: clinical trials, chemotherapy, targeted therapies. Clinical trials are becoming harder for me to qualify for because I have already received too many different chemotherapy drugs. Most of the trials for metastatic breast cancer patients limit the number of chemotherapy agents to two. I've already had Xeloda, Taxol, Carbo, and Gemzar. I simply can't be considered for most of these trials.

Enrolling in a trial means having a "washout period" with the patient receiving no treatment at all (usually three to four weeks) before starting the protocol. This can be a precarious position to put yourself in if you have already been on a treatment that has become ineffective.

So where are things for the immediate future? For now our plan is to go through one more round of this chemo combination but do it at a higher dose and see if we can get either a response or stability at least. That will buy us a few weeks to gather information on what trials are available and what we want to do.

As far as my update for the week, I had chemo on Tuesday and I needed another shot of Neulasta yesterday to boost my white count and thereby restore my infection-fighting capability. The chemo now knocks that down every time and I can't recover on my own. Once again I will need a transfusion of red blood cells tomorrow because my hemoglobin level is too low. When this happens I don't have enough oxygen-carrying capability in my blood to allow me to function normally. I get short of breath just walking or standing.

This is a predictable part of some types of chemotherapy if you are on them long enough. After enough cycles of constant chemo the body just can't compensate for what is killed in the collateral damage of treatment. Not all chemos do this, but mine does.

So the news is not what we want. It's hard to hear. This chemo combination did a great job at shrinking many lesions in a short time. I am functioning in a much better place than I was this spring, but now I worry that things will progress quickly before we find something new that works. I wonder what will work. I wonder how long it will take to find it, and what kind of shape I will be in when we do. If we do. At this point there are enough options that I do still think it's *when*, not *if*. But this day has come sooner than I'd hoped.

August 28, 2014

In Sickness and in Health: My Mother's Perspective on Reading My Blog Posts About Metastatic Cancer

I am Lisa's proud mother and I have followed her blog from its first day. As her mother, I read her blog from a unique point of view, and I want to share my perspective with you.

Those of you who are reading this blog follow Lisa and her incredible writing. It is her understanding of human behavior, her expression of feelings of her heart and thoughts of her mind that make so many people want another blog from her as soon as the one being read is finished.

Yet, as the mother of this outstanding-in-all-aspects daughter, my reading of Lisa's blog posts is complicated because each piece contains an extra layer of heart-wrenching pain for me. Lisa's blog is a precious sharing of her everyday life, of medical explanation and analysis of each and every test result, of measured consideration of her hopes, fears, etc. Parents rarely get the opportunity to get "up close and personal" to this extent with a child. As Lisa's mother, knowing her innermost thoughts is a gift and a curse.

If you (or anyone else but Lisa) were writing about a life journey with a cancer diagnosis, I could handle reading about the physical assaults on your body and the emotional assaults on your psyche because I would be more objective and not involved in your everyday life. I could read your blog, feel empathy and sorrow for the diagnosis, but step away from it. However, I am enmeshed in Lisa's writing.

I have the ambivalent feelings of wanting to be close and share every moment of what Lisa thinks and feels at that moment versus retreating from the declarations of how her life is now and her fears for the future for her and the family—her family and my family.

Lisa and I share the personality trait of always wanting to know the truth so we are as well prepared for the worst as we can be. Lisa and I promised each other that we would never withhold any information to protect each other. The honesty Lisa promised me is the honesty she has promised to all of you, her readers.

On one level, her blog reveals to me everything I want to know, but on another level what I unconsciously don't want to know. This emotional see-saw of wanting to read it but not wanting to read it is a decision that I must make each time a new blog post appears in my inbox.

Why is this "to know or not to know" decision so difficult for me? When I read Lisa's writings, I imagine the sub-text that she does not reveal: how she is managing to keep her family's lives as "normal" (whatever that means) as possible.

Lisa is, as most mothers are, the hub of her family's life. When Lisa writes in a blog post that she was very tired and rested for hours, I know that her closed bedroom door makes every family member who sees that closed door go into overdrive with founded or unfounded concern and fear.

Lisa and I share the goals to make the most of each day and to cherish and to love one another. These are life affirmations within our control when so much of life is out of our control. Lisa's readers, I invite you to join us in this goal of making the most of each day, and to share with me Lisa's greatest gift: who she is and how she lives her life, in sickness and in health.

May 10, 2013

On Grieving

Death makes people so uncomfortable. They don't even want to talk about MY death (not imminent in any way to my knowledge) much less their own. But to deny the fact that some of us live in fear constantly, and must contemplate our own mortality on a constant basis, is so patronizing.

To imply that our fears, our worries about ourselves and loved ones is unfounded is to call us irrational. Well, anyone who's had done to them what we've had done has earned that right. So if a mother of a child who has had leukemia is nervous over a fever or a doctor's visit, or a breast cancer survivor is worried over bone aches, don't say to them, "I'm sure it's nothing."

Say instead, "I'm sorry you are having to go through this. I'm sorry this is happening to you. I'm sorry that worry is so much a part of your daily life. I care about you and will be here for you." Those words are always appropriate.

September 16, 2012

Onward

It does not matter how healthy you look. It does not matter if your hair is growing back or you walk a little faster or manage with just one nap a day now.

It does not matter if any of those things are true, your cancer can be worsening.

As I have described here before, metastatic breast cancer is characterized by resistance to therapies. If a treatment works in the first place (and according to my oncologist, most have about a 30% chance of initial success), the cancer will almost certainly become resistant to it and it will cease working. This resistance will happen time after time. This has happened numerous times to me already. I have had some treatments not work at all while others worked for a few months and then would not work any longer.

Once again, this resistance has happened. It is time to move on.

Moving on is scary. It means being in freefall as we use educated guesswork to decide what agent(s) to try next.

I've known for the last week that things were probably over for this chemo. We had tried a higher dose of both drugs already without success. I adjusted to the news over the weekend and yesterday I started on a new chemotherapy regimen. We are initially planning on a schedule of two weeks on, one week off, but that may change as we go. And of course, if it isn't working, we'll have to try something else.

I'm having some other problems now that the cancer is growing so that has been a challenge. Side effects don't just stop the minute you stop taking a drug. And moving right on to another one means there is no break. It is what is needed though.

Metastatic breast cancer is like Whack-a-Mole: cancer pops up in places and then can often be whacked back down. If you're lucky you can play this game for a little while as it takes up residence in different bones and organs. We'll see how successful we are this time. This is always the hardest time for me mentally: living with the uncertainty of trying to find a new regimen, trying to find something that works, knowing right now there is nothing.

But this is the choice I have made in choosing to treat my cancer. That is the nature of this disease. These are not heroic measures. This is what treating metastatic breast cancer is.

And so we go . . . onward.

October 8, 2014

Fugitive

I know I'm supposed to stop and smell the roses
But life is going to keep moving on
Without me.

So maybe instead you should just
Keep the motor running,
Let me hop out for just a moment.

While you're not looking
I might just try to run.

But I realize you're not paying attention any more . . .
I'm taking too long,

So I will linger awhile,
Taking in the glory,
Before the last breath

September 18, 2014

Some Days I Don't

Some days I don't
Feel like a gift,
Do much,
Go anywhere,
Want to do this.

Some days I don't
Know how to get out,
Or want to be the brave one,
Be the strong one.

Some days I don't
Have any words,
Or the strength to take them from my head
And put them on a screen.

Some days I don't
Believe that this is what my life is,
What it has come to,
Or even think I have woken up for the day.

Some days I don't
Wish to believe the best days are over,
Know if the adventures have ended,
Want to believe that it can be true that they are.

But even on the days I don't . . .

Somewhere inside I know I must
Press onward,

For whatever that means,
For right now.

So every day that is just what I do.

November 14, 2014

Fall 2014

November 2

I'm not feeling that well and have been primarily staying home for the last month. Now that I think about it, though, I've been basically staying home for the last ten months. Many days my half-hour in the morning driving the older two kids to school is my only outing of the day. But I am patient.

At this point the options are still very reasonable and typical for this stage of the disease. I'm waiting for the next treatment proposal and then onward we go.

November 5

We have some big decisions to make including what chemo to go to next. First I need to deal with these more pressing issues of the liver and the heart. I had hoped to be able to rest and get through these difficult post-chemo days at home but the appointments mean pushing myself beyond what I really think I'm able to do sometimes. But I have to get answers and be able to get scheduled for what I need when I am hopefully feeling a bit better next week.

Once we have some decisions made about it all I will report back. Things just don't seem to go the easy or simple route and I'm getting used to that. For now I am going to try to conserve energy and stay pretty quiet. Thanks to you all for your continued support.

November 7

This week has been one of disappointment and adjustment. The liver situation is serious. The cancer is growing rapidly there and we need to get it under control. So, there is a lot of adjustment right now. I feel sadness, disappointment, and anger that chemo has worked so well in some areas but the liver has been resistant. Things change so fast with this disease. One day things are relatively stable and within weeks they can be spiraling out of control. As always, I will continue to educate and do what I can to show what my life with metastatic breast cancer is, what life with the disease can be.

November 19

The past week was already one of the most challenging I've had this year: my first infusion last week of a triple dose of Cisplatin had me down for the count while I was also digesting the news of the growing liver metastases and what needs to be done to try to reduce those.

As a result of the PET scan we got some additional information and what we got was not good. Obviously that isn't a surprise given that my bloodwork had already told us the prior chemos had stopped working and the cancer has been progressing. The PET confirmed that my liver is an area of increasing trouble with tumors multiplying and growing in size. Not surprising.

Also as we suspected, the fluid around my heart appears to be malignant. Then there were surprises: apparently at least one malignant lesion in my brain and new cancerous areas throughout my skull and jaw. For now we proceed with the liver plan because that is a local therapy designed to work on just that issue.

Sometimes I wonder how I walk around knowing what is in me and what it is doing to me and still manage to get through the day. I have seen the roller coaster of what this disease does. Some things that sound terrifying end up being able to be managed.

We will be scheduling chemo intermixed with my liver procedures, adjusting the chemo doses to lower ones so that there is time for my blood counts to rise in the time needed. It will be an art and science to balance.

While all of this goes on I still search for that laugh, I still appreciate the small things.

Most people know my "bit of beauty" tweet by now ("Find a bit of beauty in the world today. Share it. If you can't find it, create it. Some days this may be hard to do. Persevere."). I know that this is the quote many people will remember me for most. But I have another tweet I like to send out. Some days this one just feels right. It is:

Make the most of this day. Whatever that means to you, whatever you can do, no matter how small it seems.

For now, and again, I say: Onward.

November 24

The brain MRI on Friday unfortunately showed that the metastases are to my brain, not just my skull. I will need whole brain radiation to try to shrink them all before they cause me to have symptoms.

Whole brain radiation will radiate all of my brain tissue, healthy and malignant. It is usually given in a series of ten to fifteen sessions, every weekday. It has side effects both short term and long term. In addition there is a claustrophobia-inducing session of mask-fitting where a mold of the face and head must be made for the patient to wear during radiation treatments to immobilize them.

The most serious side effect will be fatigue. As in: sleep twenty or more hours a day fatigue. Can't get out of bed fatigue. So I will need to make arrangements to get more help here at home to help with the kids and with driving.

For now that's all I'm going to report because I want to see what the team says about my particular case and let everyone know the plan for me. It's obviously not the news I was hoping for. But as always I will do what needs to be done to try to manage it.

December 3

Things have been very busy with getting my whole brain radiation going. I've spent so much time at Sloan Kettering... yesterday I was there for seven hours.

December 11

These are very rough days. Finishing whole brain radiation tomorrow (Friday), have completed one week of liver radiation and have one more week to go. Immediately after I complete those (Christmas week) I will go back to systemic IV chemotherapy.

You always have to be willing to adjust to what the day brings and what the best new course of action is.

For now I have side effects of being wobbly, absolutely fatigued (unable to walk well or move), dehydrated, pain, and nausea. It hasn't gotten to the worst point it will and we are managing medications each day to deal with each day's issues.

I have been at MSK for IV fluids and magnesium four days this week, radiation for five days this week, and tomorrow I will even then need to head down to NYC for platelets for clotting and red cells to combat my anemia. We need these numbers to be up so I can continue radiation and then get right into chemotherapy again.

I'm not functional for the most part and the days are very tough. But I know this is what needs to happen before I can get my strength back and the cancer under control. These are important weeks and months.

That's all I have energy to report for right now, thank you for the support.

December 27

I'm thrilled that my family has gone away on vacation starting today and they will have a week to ski and be with cousins and grandparents and get a fun break while I recover here. I insisted that they go; it is so important for me to know that our kids and my husband can have some vacation time and get a break. It is not easy to be a family member/caretaker under these conditions so it gives me a lot of joy that they can have a change of scenery. I have my dad staying with me since I can't be alone and so that will work out just fine in terms of appointments and help with my needs.

Many thanks as always to those who support me daily with tweets, emails, rides to appointments, donations to my research fund, meals, etc. And to any MSKCC staff who are reading this: you know how much I adore you.

I am grateful that you all continue to join me here. Wishing you a happy and healthy new year if possible and we'll keep on going into 2015 the best we can . . .

xo,
Lisa

Anxious for Spring

Hi everyone . . . finally an update. I know I have been quiet. As you probably assumed, it has been a very difficult month. I finished whole brain radiation (and I needed to add the C2 vertebrae) and liver radiation a month ago. The brain and liver were two-week regimens each but the start times were staggered so it took three weeks to complete. I was having trouble with my magnesium and potassium levels and those needed to be addressed. As a result I needed to be at Sloan Kettering every weekday for more than thirty straight days between radiation and the aftermath. It was quite a schedule.

In the last few weeks my problem became swelling (edema) from inflammation from the liver radiation. My abdomen was shockingly distended and that was causing me trouble with discomfort and moving around.

I have had fatigue but it hasn't been the sleeping-all-day form that I was warned might happen with the brain radiation. Fatigue encompasses more than just "tiredness." For me the fatigue has been more weighted on weakness. I have had a lot of trouble walking and doing steps. I've needed to use a wheelchair at SK for a few weeks now. That shouldn't last much longer as I get stronger to walk distances again. But on the bad days I couldn't get more than down to the car for my ride.

The magnesium and potassium as of this week are finally holding with home management and no IV supplementation. A helpful tip: the low sodium form of V8 has huge quantities of potassium.

I only needed to go to Sloan Kettering for one trip this week. I do not have pain beyond what is caused by the fluid around the liver. I do not take any pain pills and haven't needed them during radiation. I have not had any headaches or neurological issues yet from the brain radiation which is probably due to the fact that my lesions were so small and the low dose of steroids. I am still winning a bunch of my Words with Friends games too! The last time I was able to leave the house to go somewhere except to go to Sloan Kettering was Thanksgiving. That boggles my mind.

I think this week has been a turning point. I am hopeful the major acute radiation effects are waning. No clue what lies ahead with the delayed ones but I don't focus on that. For now I will be working on strength (after being basically bedridden for a month) and trying to get more function back. It is a process.

If all goes well I will start a new chemo cycle next week. Each day is different and I can't predict how I will feel. But that seems to be the way life will be for me now. I long ago adjusted to that.

I am grateful for all of the support and concern shown over the last month from you. I understandably wasn't able to return many messages. This past month was really about just getting through. The energy I did have was spent making sure the kids were able to maintain their usual schedules and we made it. Friends who have helped with rides and meals: thank you.

I'm already anxious for spring to get here. Xo

January 17, 2015

Making Tough Days Better

Most of the last three weeks since I last wrote have been dealing still with swelling and blood count issues from radiation and from the extensive disease in my liver that we are working on with the radiation and with chemo. I've needed numerous transfusions of red cells for anemia and quite a few for platelets which have really come under attack. Rather than being cytotoxic chemos (traditional "cell-killers") these are anti-hormonal agents. We are just trying to let my body recover now for a few weeks.

Last week my abdomen grew and grew with fluid from the liver and overall inflammation. By the end of the week I had an abdomen the size I was when I was ready to give birth. The skin was painfully stretched. We needed to intervene. I went to urgent care for evaluation for a paracentesis (draining/"tap" of fluid). Two and one half liters later we were done. It is a huge amount to see. I did have soreness at the site and discomfort from such a lot of fluid removal after. But this is a very common procedure with metastases to the liver.

(Please, please remember: breast cancer that metastasizes to the liver is not liver cancer. Mets [metastases] to the brain are not brain cancer. They are breast cancer cells that have moved in the body. There can be/are big differences in terms of prognosis, treatment, chemotherapy agents, etc.)

We are working on the plan for next week; it is likely that I will be going back to a chemotherapy called Xeloda (these are pills taken daily) for a bit because it is gentler on blood counts.

I'm weak, still unable to drive, or do much more than walk to the bathroom or a car that is picking me up. I've had to adjust some things at home including bathroom rails and so on. Safety is most important and especially with very low platelets falls and any bleeding or injury risk is a serious concern.

I'm sure I've forgotten something (or things) but I do want to get this out today. I see snow out the window but I'm still focused on spring. These hydrangeas in my room this week reminded me March is not far off.

Thank you to those near and far for all different kinds of support given this month with an extra shout-out to my wonderful team at Sloan Kettering. If any of my doctors, nurses, or support staff there are reading this: you help make these tough days better. I value your care always.

February 12, 2015

No Change

Hi. Things have gotten exponentially harder in the last few weeks.

I was admitted to the hospital Wednesday and had a Tenckoff catheter put in. They removed another five liters of fluid at surgery. Now I have a catheter that allows me to drain myself at home. But, so much fluid removal in a short period messes with electrolytes, BP, etc. and makes you feel rotten until you get equilibrium.

Still cannot walk—no change predicted in short order. We are installing ramps, bought wheelchair, etc.

For now that is all I have energy to update but should give you a sense of where things are.

Xo, Lisa

March 1, 2015

On Facebook

Lisa Bonchek Adams
March 5, 2015 · Darien, CT · 🏛 ▾

Things are very serious. Please do not text daily. I cannot answer most of time

👍 Like   💬 Comment   ➦ Share   ⬙ Buffer

In Memorium—March 6, 2015

The thousands upon thousands who knew and loved Lisa Bonchek Adams; whether in person or via Facebook, Twitter, or her website and blog read around the world; whether up close or from afar; will find it hard to believe that her steely will and indomitable spirit were finally overcome by the disease she had lived with for so many years.

Lisa died at home around 9:45 p.m. on Friday, March 6, 2015, surrounded by her entire family.

Lisa was cared for to the end by her beloved Dr. Chau Dang of Memorial Sloan Kettering Cancer Center.

The Adams and Bonchek families send a heartfelt thank you to all for your love and support. We know that Lisa will always be a part of your lives, as she will be a part of ours.

FINAL THOUGHTS

I'm Sorry

I'll apologize for anything. I'll apologize for other people's actions. I'll apologize for the bad weather we're having or your migraine or the fact you backed your car into a stone wall.

I'll apologize for having cancer. I'll apologize for the fact that through no fault of my own I'm going to die and leave my children motherless at a young age.

It's not that I think it's my fault; it's that I wish it could be different. I am sorry; it's true.

To my husband:

I'm sorry I am leaving you with this mess. I'm sorry I am leaving you a single parent. I'm sorry I won't be here to share not only the good times, but the bad times, too. I am sorry I won't be here to share the load. It's not easy raising children. I wish I could be here to help for longer.

I'm sorry you will have to do so much without me. I'm sorry you will have to pay the bills and put potassium in the water softener and clean up the dishes and remember to turn the sprinkler system off for the winter. I'm sorry you will have to remember to give the dog her monthly pill and schedule dental visits for the kids and that the outdoor light settings need to be changed with daylight savings time.

There are one thousand things I need to write down for you to remember. I am sorry I won't be able to just do them for you instead.

I'm sorry that I have been the sick one. I'm sorry you have given me "for better"' while I have given you "for worse." I know I would do for you what I will be asking you to do for me. I am sorry that I will not grow old with you. I'm sorry we'll never do the things we thought we would.

You deserved more than this. I guess I think I did, too. I know there is no justice meter in this world. Our lives are proof it's true.

I'm sorry you will have to do things without me. Our children's weddings, graduations, birthdays, Christmases. I'm sorry there will be sadness with each of them when I am not here to share them.

I'm sorry I won't be here to sit in bed next to you and read quietly. I'm sorry our years of loving one another will be fewer. I'm sorry you will see me sick, weak, suffering. I am sorry our children will see that too.

To my friends:

I am sorry. I am sorry I won't be here more to help you when you have your own health problems. I'm sorry I won't be a resource for you or friend to support you. I'm sorry it will be mostly a one way street from here on out. I will need you more than you need me. My family will need you, too, after I'm gone.

Please help them. Know they are hurting. Talk to my children about me. Let them talk to you about me. Share stories, tell them things I did that helped others. Tell a joke, a funny secret, something they might not have known.

To my children:

There is no greater apology I can offer you than to say that if I could do anything, anything in this world to be here longer with you I would. People tell me I should "stay strong" and "fight the good fight" and "kick cancer's ass." When I die it will not be because I didn't do those things. My death will not be because I didn't try hard enough or have a good attitude.

When I die it will be because we don't understand this disease. Because we don't know enough about metastatic breast cancer. Because these cells divided faster than I could kill them with chemo and were sneakier and trickier to mutate and become resistant to everything I tried.

I removed my breasts, my ovaries, and did everything I possibly could to try to maximize my life here on earth. But sometimes doing everything you possibly can just isn't enough. I am sorry to tell you that is the truth.

The world is unfair, my darlings. That's the truth too. It's cold and cruel and harsh and unfair.

But it's also wonderful and beautiful and gentle and kind. And I have gotten back in these last years what I have given. Helping others is important. Not because you want something in return, but just because it's right. Give money to charity. Help others not only financially if you can, but with your time, and with your heart. I have poured out as much as I can to others, and know it has mattered to them and to me.

Do not remember me in pain or weakened from this wicked disease. Please remember me doing what I loved most: being your mom. Look at photos and see my beaming face, my smile, my twinkling eyes. Remember how you made me feel. How I loved you. How proud you made me each and every single day.

Remember the happy times, remember the laughter. It's important to remember the sadness too, I suppose. You must remember the pain and sadness to have compassion for others. But please know that what crushes me to the core is the thought of your needing me and my not being there for you. That is a parent's nightmare.

Yes, I know people do it every day. I know mothers die. I know they leave their children. I never thought this is how my life would end. I never could have imagined this chapter. I know children are resilient. I know you will still grow and mature and develop into caring, smart, talented adults. I have hopefully instilled enough in you to get you started on this path. But damn it, I wish I could see it all.

Don't you dare think of me as a pessimist. Don't think I was a negative person. There is a difference between realism and pessimism. Think of me as a straight-talker. Think of me as honest, even when it hurts. Read my words. Read my blog posts. You will know me forever through my words and we can still have a relationship even after I am dead. This doesn't mean I will be looking down on you from heaven (you know I don't believe in that) or that I will be an angel or any of those things that I also don't believe are true. I wish they were, dear ones.

But we can still have a relationship. You can still think of me, predict what I would say, remember me. Our relationship will continue on in your minds. The same way I think of Grandma and she is still a part of my life—her love and her life are still in mine—that is what will happen for you with me.

Read my words. They are my legacy to you. They are my dying wishes. They are my hopes and dreams and sorrows and rants.

I am sorry I could not be here for you for longer, not only for yourself but also for me. You bring me so much joy. I may have been strict and hard on you but you must understand I had a lot of teaching to get into a short amount of time. Remember your manners. Remember to think of others. Remember that doing good things feels good. There is intrinsic value in being ethical.

Take care of one another, please. Love each other as you always have. Reminisce about me and tell funny stories. Be each other's support system when you can.

Life does go on, whether we like it or not. Grief will come back again and again for the rest of your lives. That's normal. But do not get bogged down by it if you can. You will learn to incorporate my absence into your lives.

Somehow you will. But memories will jump out at you and shock you when you least expect it. A song, a smell, a flower . . . you will see me in places you least expect. Think of me fondly then. Think of me with love. Know that my love for you does not end when my life does.

I could go on forever like this, you see. I will apologize for anything. I will spend time being sorry for the pain I am going to inflict on you all. But that is part of life. That is what this is.

My job is to teach you the skills you need to deal with what gets thrown at you. Coping skills. Resilience. Determination. I hope that I have been an example of how to deal with what is commonly called "the bum rap." I hope you remember my strength, my devotion, my tenacity. I hope you are learning how to be resilient. This doesn't mean ignoring pain or sadness. No way.

It means learning how to accept what IS and moving forward anyway.

I'm sorry I could not do it all. I'm sorry I could not be better. I'm sorry that I have this disease.

That's me. I told you: I'll apologize for anything.

February 1, 2013

When I Die

When I die don't think you've "lost" me.
I'll be right there with you, living on in the memories we have made.

When I die don't say I "fought a battle." Or "lost a battle." Or "succumbed."
Don't make it sound like I didn't try hard enough, or have the right attitude, or that I simply gave up.

When I die don't say I "passed."
That sounds like I walked by you in the corridor at school.

When I die tell the world what happened.

Plain and simple.
No euphemisms, no flowery language, no metaphors.

Instead, remember me and let my words live on.

Tell stories of something good I did.

Give my children a kind word. Let them know what they meant to me. That I would have stayed forever if I could.

Don't try to comfort my children by telling them I'm an angel watching over them from heaven or that I'm in a better place:

There is no better place to me than being here with them. They have learned about grief and they will learn more.

That is part of it all.

When I die someday just tell the truth:
I lived, I died.
The end.

July 13, 2012

EULOGIES

Eulogy by Lisa's Husband, Clarke D. Adams

What I think made Lisa special and so loved was her compassion and empathy. From the very beginning of our relationship she was drawn to people who had experienced suffering or adversity in their lives. We always joked she should have been a physician or a therapist since she played one (unpaid I might add) in her daily life anyway. If you needed a friend she was there with advice or an offer to help or just a bowl of soup or a kind word. She was an extraordinary friend and even when things were extremely tough for her she was giving of herself to me, to our children, and to her friends who she held dear.

I believe the story that really captured the essence of what Lisa was all about was the birth of our youngest, Tristan. I had been through the whole childbirth thing twice before so was feeling confident that I was an old pro and would get through it OK. However, my confidence proved unwarranted.

About forty minutes into the delivery when things were getting pretty intense the doctor looked up at me and said, "I don't like the look of dad . . . get somebody in here quickly." At that point I was pale and sweaty and on the precipice of losing consciousness which had also nearly happened during Paige's birth. The ob-gyn and a swarm of nurses began tending to me, got me a chair and began rubbing my shoulders and sponging my brow and altogether ignoring Lisa who was giving birth right next to us.

I would have thought she would have been justifiably annoyed with me. However, that wasn't her. Right at that moment, probably five minutes before Tristan was born, Lisa was reaching out to me, stroking my hair and comforting me and telling me it was ok and all with a smile, a laugh, and an attitude of amusement and appreciation for the absurdity of the situation.

That was her nature . . . she gave of herself to others: her time, her friendship, her love, her good humor, and her intellect and ability, and she did it with the same intensity, effort, and sincerity when things were difficult for her as when they were good.

When she got sick she transferred that same passion to her writing and her blogging. At first she just wrote as a therapeutic exercise and a vehicle to explore her feelings and experiences. Gradually, people all over the country and really the world, person by person and totally by word of mouth, discovered her writing and responded to it.

Over the course of the last six years she built a passionate following and circle of friends. She felt that it was her responsibility to help educate and demystify what it meant to be a young mom and have breast cancer and later what it meant to be a young mom and have metastatic breast cancer. She also wrote beautifully on the themes of grief, loss, and family.

I have heard from dozens of men and women who followed Lisa on the web and on Twitter. Her writing was clear, concise, and heartfelt. But what I think people responded to most was that she cared for the individual. If you emailed her she would write back. If you called she would speak to you for hours. She would answer questions in online forums on the Internet until late at night. She genuinely cared about those who reached out to her, and she wanted to help. It is no surprise to me then that the community of her friends and readers has been there for her when she needed help the most and for that we are thankful. For Lisa it all came back to her loved ones and especially the family.

Things got very tough for her in the last week of her life. When she was able to speak she spoke of how sad she was to leave but also of how proud she was of the kids. Tristan, Paige, and Colin, she loved you completely and her very last words to me were of how lucky she was to have been your mother and how her only regret was she wouldn't get to enjoy seeing you guys finish growing up. She knew though that you were going to be great.

I had a sweet moment when Paige and I were going through her things. Two boxes appeared at our door the Tuesday after she died. We opened them and inside were presents for Tristan's ninth birthday... I checked her Amazon account... she had ordered them Wednesday evening when she knew things were getting very serious. One of her very last conscious acts was as a mom thinking of her youngest. She took a few of her precious remaining minutes to make sure that Tristan had something nice on his birthday.

That was just who she was. She gave of herself to those she loved and the world is a better place for her having been in it if only for a short time... that is the only epitaph worth having and Lisa's is a life that is worth remembering, celebrating, and honoring. We shall miss her very much.

Eulogy by Lisa's Daughter, Paige Adams

My mum always said to find a bit of beauty in the world. She said to seek it out, to cherish it, to preserve it in its entirety.

To me, my mum was that bit of beauty.

She was the kind of person that everyone wanted to make happy. People were constantly sending her gifts, flowers, cards... everyone adored, and still adores, her, myself included. She was such a big part of my life that it's hard to believe that she's gone.

I never made a decision, big or small, without having her behind me, and she always was. Everything I did, I had her full support. She was compassionate but stern, a friend and a parent, the eternal voice of reason, and the best mum you could ask for.

When I said I wanted to take up kickboxing, I was signed up for classes the next day. When I decided to take up acting, she helped me practice an audition. And, in the fourth grade, when I was convinced that it was my destiny to go to Yale (then Stanford, then Harvard, then Princeton), she was convinced too.

Now, she was nothing if not a realist, but more so, she was a believer. She believed in me, but she also believed in herself. And personally, I think the power of such a belief is what made her the anomaly in making it as far as she did.

On my eleventh birthday, she wrote:

*I hope I will have many more years to watch you grow
and see what you will do in the years ahead.*

*You make me proud,
you make me smile,
you make me laugh,
you make me cry.*

*Now, forever and always,
I believe in you.*

*May you someday know the joy that I have known having you
as my daughter and the special bond we will always share.*

I'm not exactly sure why she said I made her cry, but I hope it
was just poetic license. The point is, not many people my age
get to appreciate the bond that they have with their mothers.
We were there for each other. I can only imagine how hard it
is to be a mother without everything she had to go through,
and every day I appreciate her altruism, valiance, and loyalty
for my family and me. She knew how much I loved her, and,
more importantly, I knew how much she loved me: something
that not many people can acknowledge and appreciate daily in
their own parents.

More than once, she called herself a quitter, but I can tell you
firsthand that she was the one person who never gave up.

Eulogy by Lisa's Father, Dr. Lawrence Bonchek

Lisa, we hardly knew you.

Living with Lisa since her diagnosis in 2006 was a learning experience—we learned about a Lisa we did not previously know.

During her teens there were early signs of the ferocious willpower that flourished later, but we thought she was just being a typical teenager.

Writing was another of her skills that wasn't immediately apparent, because when I read her Master's thesis I actually could not understand the convoluted academic jargon she felt obliged to use.

Little did we know then how well she could write plain English.

When cancer struck, Lisa's unflinching writing about it introduced us to someone we did not yet know.

William Styron, the author of Sophie's Choice, said: "true artists must paint life honestly according to their vision."

Lisa knew that instinctively. On her blog, day after day, week after week, year after year, she wrote about how what was happening in her life could teach us about living.

Cancer provokes an acute awareness of mortality that teaches life lessons about how to distinguish the vital from the trivial, and how to endure.

Lisa understood those lessons, but what really differentiated her was the ability to teach those lessons to others.

When you live with cancer, each day brings new challenges. Those cancer patients who see all the challenges as part of a single, unified whole, often find the cumulative emotional burden so oppressive and debilitating they shrink into themselves or just give up.

Lisa didn't. For her, chronicling every detail of each treatment enabled her to deal with each challenge individually. She thus made them tolerable not only for herself, but for all her readers. It proved a brilliant insight, and it kept her from ever shrinking into herself or giving up.

It was as if Lisa got up each morning to go to work, but just happened to have an unpleasant job. Being treated for cancer was her job and, doggedly, relentlessly, she just did what had to be done—chemotherapy, having an intravenous port inserted, getting her brain irradiated, whatever...

When we look back at the cumulative burden of what Lisa endured through the years without complaining, we are astonished by her tenacity and feistiness, her sheer grit and determination to just keep going, because the paycheck for that unpleasant job of hers was more time with the family she loved.

She made striving to stay alive meaningful, because she had reasons to live. They are called Clarke, Paige, Colin, and Tristan.

As all her readers know, her love was always turned outward. Over the break for Christmas 2014, I stayed with her because otherwise Clarke wouldn't leave her to take the family for their annual skiing vacation in Wyoming with his large family. At the time, Lisa and I reminisced that when she and Mark were little, Rita and I thought the baby sitters ought to be board-certified pediatricians. It amused us to think that now Lisa had gone us one better and had a sitter who was a board-certified heart surgeon.

Lisa—it's clear now that when all this started we hardly knew you. But, with thousands of others, we learned a lot about you. Sure, anyone could see you had a fierce will, but thousands of others found that your will was wrapped up in other qualities. As one follower wrote, you were also "warm, thoughtful, gracious, dignified, devastatingly candid, and so brave."

For all of us with aching hearts, I'll conclude with some lines by an anonymous poet:

> *"Those we love don't go away,*
> *They walk beside us every day.*
> *Unseen—unheard, but always here.*
> *Still loved, still missed, still very dear."*

MEDICAL

About My Cancer

In December of 2006 I visited my ob-gyn for my six-month post-partum visit after the birth of my third child, Tristan. Eighteen months after a clear mammogram (done at age thirty-six when my mother had been diagnosed with breast cancer), my doctor did a breast check and said one side felt "different" than the other. No palpable lump, just different density. Neither of us was worried, but she got me in for the repeat mammogram and ultrasound the week before Christmas.

At that visit, I was told I had extensive DCIS (ductal carcinoma in situ) in my left breast. It was unclear if I had any invasive cancer as well; none showed up on the mammogram and ultrasound. I would need a biopsy to try to answer this question. This was not possible before Christmas. I would have to wait more than two weeks for that biopsy.

After that biopsy I was told I "only" had DCIS; no invasive cancer was present in the sample. I needed a mastectomy because the DCIS was widespread. After consulting with my surgical oncologist and reconstructive surgeon, I decided to have a bilateral mastectomy both for aesthetic and prophylactic reasons.

After my double mastectomy and sentinel node biopsy I was told that there was no cancer in my lymph nodes. However, this original pathology report was wrong (not uncommon with a micro-metastasis). Two to three weeks later I received a call that the slides were reviewed again and in fact, I did have a micro-metastasis to a lymph node. I would need chemotherapy.

A few weeks after that phone call, when I received a second opinion about chemotherapy regimens, a different set of pathologists found two small tumors of invasive ductal carcinoma in the samples taken when my left breast was removed. These tumors were not large enough to be visible on mammogram or ultrasound.

Therefore despite believing I had extensive DCIS, I actually had stage II, grade 3 invasive ductal carcinoma that had spread to one lymph node. My decision to have a bilateral mastectomy had been a good choice for me, and saved me from needing further surgery.

I received tissue expanders to begin the reconstruction process. I was able to wake up to expanders filled with about half of their final volume. I finished all of my expander fills prior to chemo.

I started chemotherapy six weeks after my surgery on a dose-dense schedule. I received four rounds of Adriamycin and Cytoxan two weeks apart followed by four rounds of Taxol two weeks apart.

One month after finishing chemo I had surgery to swap my expanders for silicone implants. Later procedures gave me surgically constructed nipples and areola pigment.

After my menstrual period returned following chemotherapy, I began taking Zoladex injections to suppress my ovarian function (at these injections, a pellet of medication is inserted in abdominal fat that dissolves slowly over one month). With Er+, Pr+ cancer, I did not want the hormone fluctuations of menstruation.

In December of 2008 I had a salpingo-oophorectomy (removal of my Fallopian tubes and ovaries).

Unfortunately, in October of 2012 I learned my breast cancer had metastasized to my bones. I now have stage IV cancer.

The first regimen I tried was Xeloda oral chemo. I was on a one week on/one week off routine. I took 4000 mg each day of my "on" week (eight pills). I also received monthly infusions of Zometa. In January of 2013 I had to stop Zometa because of negative side effects and switched successfully to Xgeva injections which I tolerate much better.

In April of 2013, though the Xeloda did shrink my cancer (confirmed via PET scan), it stopped working. My tumor markers were slowly rising. I needed to try something else. I started a new cocktail of Aromasin and Afinitor and continued with the monthly Xgeva injections.

In September of 2013 the Aromasin/Afinitor combo again stopped working.

On October 28, 2013, I enrolled in a clinical trial of a Pi3k inhibitor plus Faslodex. The investigational drug was called GDC-0032 and is made by Genentech. I continued with monthly Xgeva injections as well.

In December 2013 we learned that the clinical trial regimen was not working.

In January 2014 I was hospitalized for three weeks and during this time I had a PleurX lung drain put in (removed after two weeks) and ten sessions of radiation to my hips and spine.

I also had genomic testing which uncovered many mutations including ESR1. Of course we do not know in all of those mutations which are significant and which are just incidental findings. We now have the ability to detect mutations that far exceed our ability to override or correct them. We don't know exactly how the mutations interact and which ones dominate others. Breast cancer is a complicated disease. This is why we don't have the cure we've been promised for decades.

I began Taxol infusions in January 2014 but in March we learned the Taxol was not working. The cancer was significantly worse.

In March 2014 I began Carboplatin and Gemzar and immediately my tumor markers indicated this combo was working. In September 2014 the Carbo/Gem combo stopped working.

In October 2014 I began Navelbine at my next chemotherapy.

I am thankful for the doctors and scientists who provide me with medications, personal guidance, and research to rationally fight that which ails me.

I am grateful for my loving husband, Clarke, my three children (now ages sixteen, twelve, and eight), parents, friends, doctors, and my readers who have supported me and my chronicle here.

I'm glad you are joining me . . . Everything is better with a friend.

Eye to Eye: The Doctor-Patient Relationship in Stage IV Cancer

Everything changes with a diagnosis of Stage 4 cancer. I don't really think that's an overstatement. My relationship with my oncologists has, by nature, changed as well. With stage 4 one of the things that's especially important is good communication between physician and patient.

Immediately after I was diagnosed in October with stage IV my oncologists began talking about finding a balance between length of life and quality of life. These two aspects of my life would have to be constantly juggled.

For many people it is often reassuring to hear there is a plan, a prescribed protocol. There is a type of comfort in being diagnosed with a disease and being told there are defined steps you need to take. With metastatic cancer it's not crystal clear. Patients must often help decide what is right for them.

When I went to see my medical oncologist at Sloan Kettering this week, she pulled the chair over and sat only inches from me. I was on the exam table, in the modest red and peach Seersucker bathrobe Sloan uses for their exam gowns. We sat and talked about research and trials and side effects and my blog and my family. She gets emotional sometimes when we talk about the current situation. So do I.

Then Dr. Chau Dang said something that I will always remember. She said that many doctors start to distance themselves from their patients as the patients get sicker and closer to death. She said this is their coping mechanism. Of course I couldn't help but wonder if the same process is what is behind some of my friends disappearing and rarely contacting me anymore. Some physicians, she said, seem to back away, needing emotional distance not to be weakened each and every time a patient dies.

In contrast, my doctor feels this is precisely the time in her relationship with her patients to embrace them, bring them close, provide them care and comfort as much as possible. It's important to remember, she always says, that this isn't a case, this is a life. A person with friends and families who love them. Death happens for all of us. It's her role to do what she can to prolong life, and when that can't be done anymore, it's important to still care for the person, not just treat the disease.

The nature of the doctor-patient relationship changes over the course of illness. Perhaps nowhere is that truer than in oncology. I've always been a partner in my care, it's the only way I know how to be. It's my life, after all, and the decisions we make as a team are ones I do not want to regret because I gave up control or didn't have adequate information. However, I also accept that treating cancer is not an exact science.

Some patients do not want to have options. They want their physician to pick the course of treatment that seems best matched for the patient and proceed. A patient sometimes doesn't want choices; he or she wants the doctor to do the sifting and prescribing. This works for many people, and takes the responsibility off the patient. There is mental comfort in that approach, too. I can understand why some people make that choice.

One of the things that is difficult in being a true participant in your own care is that while you get the satisfaction of partial control, you also must accept responsibility if/when things go wrong. This is part of the deal.

Some things just are.
Some things just happen, even when you do all you can.
I have accepted this jagged truth all along.
But I think some people never do.

March 7, 2013

The Must-Have Medical Binder: The Key to Being an Organized Patient

Perhaps the most common question I get asked by email is, "Someone I know has been diagnosed with cancer. What can I do?" Today I offer one suggestion. I believe this would make a wonderful gift for someone who has just been diagnosed and is a necessity if you are the patient.

Being organized is one of the best ways to help yourself once you've been diagnosed. When you first hear the words "You have cancer" your head starts to swim. Everything gets foggy, you have to keep convincing yourself it's true.

But almost immediately decisions need to be made—decisions about doctors, treatments, and surgeries. Often these choices must be made under time constraints. You may be seeing many different doctors for consultations. Medical oncologists, surgical oncologists, radiation oncologists, reconstructive surgeons, internists—there are many different voices that you may hear, and they may be conflicting. It's hard to keep it all straight in the midst of the emotional news. Not only are you likely to be scared, but also you are suddenly thrust into a world with a whole new vocabulary. By the time you are done with it, you will feel you have mastered a second language.

You can help your care and treatment by being organized. Especially if you are juggling different specialists and different medical facilities, you must remember that the common factor in all of this is you. It's your health. It's your life. I believe it's important to travel with a binder of information about your medical history and treatment, as well as notes and questions.

This binder will mean that all of your information about your cancer will be in one place. This will be your resource guide. I cannot tell you how many times physicians have asked about my binder and said when I was able to produce test results, pathology reports, or other information they needed, "I wish every patient had one of those."

I suggest the following:

A heavy 3-ring binder

I think a 1.5" binder is a good size to start. This size will allow you to easily access reports and pages and have room for the calendar. It will look big at first but you won't believe how quickly you will fill it up.

Colored tab dividers

I like these to be erasable. I think eight is the minimum number you will need. If you have a lot of specialists you will need more. The categories you think you will need at the outset may change. It's easy to erase and reorganize them. Put the categories you will be accessing the most in the front so you aren't always having to flip to the back. Once the binder is full it will make a difference.

Some starting categories:

- schedules (Dates of appointments you have had, when the next ones are due, and how often you need certain tests done.)

- test results/pathology (It's very important to keep copies of MRI, CT, and pathology reports so that you correctly tell other doctors what your diagnosis is. For example, new patients often confuse "grade" with "stage" of cancer.)

- insurance (Keep copies of all correspondence, denial of claims, appeal letters, explanations of benefits.)

- articles and research (Handouts, post-surgical information. Ask if there are any websites your doctor does approve of. My own oncologist said, "Do not read anything about cancer on the Internet unless it comes from a source I've told you is okay. There's a lot of misinformation out there." Keep your post-surgical instructions, any info given to you about aftercare.)

- radiation/chemo (Keep records of exactly what you had done, number of sessions, dates, drug names, etc. I also asked how my dose was calculated so I knew exactly how much of each drug I received in total.)

- medications (Drug names, dates you took them, dosage, side effects. I also keep a list of all of my current medications as a "note" in my iPhone. That way I can just copy it down and won't forget anything on the list. You should always include any vitamins or supplements you take.)

- medical history (Write out your own medical history and keep it handy so that when you fill out forms asking for the information you won't forget anything. As part of it, include any relatives that had cancer. Write out what type it was, how old they were at death, and their cause of death. Also in this section include genetic test results, if relevant.)

Looseleaf paper

Perfect for note-taking at appointments, jotting down questions you have for each doctor. You can file them in the appropriate category so when you arrive at a doctor your questions are all in one place.

Business card pages

These are one of my best ideas. At every doctor's office, ask for a business card. Keep a card from every doctor you visit even if you ultimately decide not to return to them. If you have had any consultation or bloodwork there, you should have a card. That way, you will always have contact information when filling out forms at each doctor's office. For hospitals, get cards from the radiology department and medical records department so if you need to contact them you will have it. Also, you want contact information for all pathology departments that have seen slides from any biopsy you have had. You may need to contact them to have your slides sent out for a second opinion.

This is also a good place to keep your appointment reminder cards.

CD holders

At CT, MRI, or other imaging tests, ask them to burn a CD for your records. Hospitals are used to making copies for patients these days and often don't charge for it. Keep one copy for yourself of each test that you do not give away. If you need a copy to bring to a physician, get an extra made; don't give yours up. If you need to get it from medical records from the hospital, do that. You want to know you always have a copy of these images.

Keep a copy of most recent bloodwork (especially during chemo), operative notes from your surgeries (you usually have to ask for these), pathology reports, and radiology reports with interpretations of any test (MRI, CT, mammogram, etc.) you may have had. Pathology reports are vital.

Calendar

I suggest a three-hole calendar to keep in your binder. This will serve not only to keep all of your appointments in one place but also allow you to put reminders of when you need to have follow-up visits. Sometimes doctor's offices do not have their schedules set three, six, or twelve months in advance. You can put a reminder notice to yourself in the appropriate month to call ahead to check/schedule the appointment.

Similarly you can document when you had certain tests (mammograms, bone density, bloodwork) so you will have the date available. I usually keep a piece of lined paper in the "scheduling" section of my binder that lists by month and year every test/appointment that is due and also every test I've had and when I had it.

Sticky note tabs

These can be used to easily identify important papers that you will refer to often, including diagnosis and pathology. These stick on the side of the page and can be removed easily. As your binder fills up, they can be very helpful to identify your most recent bloodwork, for example.

Plastic folder sleeves

These are clear plastic sleeves that you access from the top. They can be useful for storing prescriptions or small notes that your doctor may give you. The sleeves make them easy to see/find and you won't lose the small slips of paper. Also a good place to store any lab orders that might be given to you ahead of time.

The above suggestions are a good working start to being organized during your cancer treatment. If you want to do something for a friend who is newly diagnosed, go out and buy the supplies, organize the binder and give it to your friend. He or she will most likely appreciate being given a ready-made tool to use in the difficult days ahead.

I also believe a modified version is equally useful for diagnoses other than cancer. When our youngest son was born with a medical condition it took many specialists and lots of tests to get a correct diagnosis. Having all of his tests and papers in a binder like this was instrumental in keeping his care coordinated. In fact, at his first surgery at The Children's Hospital of Pennsylvania they gave us a binder to assist in this process. I know some hospitals do this for newly diagnosed patients already. Maybe my tips will help you or a friend know how to better use the one you already have. You may not need all of these elements depending on the complexity of your case, but I hope you will find some of these suggestions useful.

January 23, 2013

CURATORS

"Death ends a life, but it does not end a relationship."

—ROBERT ANDERSON

Dr. Rita Bonchek

Lisa's mother, Dr. Rita Bonchek, is a retired therapist specializing in grief and loss. One of Lisa's wishes was to turn her writings into a book, and it has been Rita's great privilege with Mark to fulfill this wish for her.

Rita is herself a breast cancer survivor, and in 2005 she established the Rita Bonchek Cancer Care Fund as part of the Lancaster General Health Foundation in Lancaster, Pennsylvania where she lives. The fund provides financial support for wigs, head coverings and other personal care items to help women living with cancer maintain a healthy self-image.

Dr. Mark Bonchek

Lisa's brother, Dr. Mark Bonchek, is the founder of Shift Thinking. He advises leaders and organizations on digital business strategies and writes regularly for the Harvard Business Review. Mark lives in Wellesley, Massachusetts with his wife and three sons.

In the 1990s, Mark's doctoral research predicted the rise of social media. It is fitting that twenty years later, Lisa's work became a subject for the next generation of scholars—how digital connections can create very human relationships.

FINDING A CURE

"The state of metastatic breast cancer care is that you can't just test your breast cancer, look on a chart to find the drug that will work and always shut it down. We need to get aggressive in a new way now."

—Lisa Bonchek Adams,
from "We Are Not There Yet," December 18, 2013

All proceeds from the sale of *Persevere: A Life With Cancer* go towards finding a scientific solution to metastatic breast cancer.

This book was produced as an initiative of the Bonchek Family Foundation, a charitable organization created to continue Lisa's work and share her writings with a wider audience.

Additional copies of the book and donations to Lisa's research fund can be arranged through the web site of http://www.LisasBook.com

We also hope to bring greater recognition and appreciation to the remarkable people who care for those with metastatic breast cancer. Lisa had an extraordinary care team at Memorial Sloan Kettering, led by Dr. Chau Dang whose dedication, wisdom and compassion were exemplary.